MW01284560

Acknowledgments

To my beautiful bride, Caroline, who followed me across the world
and has constantly been supportive of this crazy ride. I owe you a
debt of gratitude I cannot possibly repay.

Also to Emily, Elizabeth, Madeline, Katie and Matthew.
You are my shining lights.

And to any employee who ever worked in our businesses. Some
were very memorable for all the right reasons and some for all the
wrong reasons. Unfortunately, there are some whose name I don't
quite remember. That being said, I have learned something valuable
from each of you.

Copyright © 2015 by Stephen Christensen
www.hopelesstohero.com
ISBN: 978-1500888596

All rights reserved.
No part of this book may be reproduced scanned or distributed in
any printed or electronic form without the express written
permission of the publisher. Failure to comply with these terms may
expose offenders to legal action and damages for copyright
infringement.

Cover design by Stephen Christensen
Edited by Amanda Brown

INDEX

i. Preface – My Story

I had only worked a couple of jobs in my life by the time I was thirty-five years old. My first job out of high school was what we affectionately called in Australia, a trolley boy.

My friend Adam Smith, who was doing a management internship at the Woolworths Grocery store, set me up with my first foray into the workforce. I was packing grocery bags for customers and collecting shopping carts (trolleys). It wasn't the most appealing or inspiring work and to tell you the truth it only took me two days to decide that this job was the pits. At about 3 p.m. on day two, I walked out into the parking lot to retrieve a bunch of rogue shopping carts, and upon reaching the extremities of the lot, decided to keep walking and never return.

I had learned a valuable lesson that second day. It's not worth staying in a job where you are desperately waiting for the day to end out of hatred for what you are doing or who you are doing it for.

Job number two—another set up. A friend from church worked for a national bank called Westpac and helped me get an interview for a teller's job at a local branch. It was the first real job interview I had ever been to and I was petrified. I think as an eighteen-year-old, skinny kid, I hadn't had too many experiences that prepared me for the business side of an interview desk, but I must have said something right. Within two weeks I was waiting for a bus near our home to take me to the Westpac branch at Capalaba for my first job. Yeah, OK—technically this was my second job, but at this point I was trying to bury the "trolley boy" days so deeply into my subconscious that I could convince myself that they never existed.

So back to the bus stop. There I was in my pastel green pants, pastel pink shirt and a knitted pastel lemon tie with the straight bottom (this was 1985 after all), when a freak thunderstorm formed over the very spot I was waiting for the bus. With no cover in sight, I was drenched from head to toe when the bus showed up. Rather than be late for my first day, I squelched down the aisle to the back seat and sat down—water pooling around my seat from my clothing. I thought, *This is a nice way to show up for my first day at work, wearing a pastel swamp.*

There was a large shopping mall across the road from the bank. Being somewhat early, I went into Kmart for the purpose of buying something to dry off with, but I only had a dollar or two in my pocket. All I could afford was a tea towel, but I bought it anyway and walked across the road rubbing my hair and my clothes vigorously with said towel. By the time I had reached the door of the bank, my hair was standing on end and the crumpled and damp clothes probably defined what sort of employee my new boss thought I would be.

I remember knocking on the door. The rest of the staff were having a meeting and each one of them turned to look at their new colleague—the new team member, the new customer service officer who would represent the bank to its customers. I'm sure they were well disappointed.

I enjoyed my next two years at the bank. There were about twenty teller stations, and I was the only male teller. By far the best lesson I had learned was that regardless of how competent I was as a cash handler or financial auditor, having great customer service skills always kept my customers happy. I learned that connecting with the customer was by far the number one priority in any business, whether it was opening a savings account or scooping a chocolate dipped waffle cone.

I left the bank to pursue a goal I had set for myself years earlier and served a two-year mission for the Church of Jesus Christ of Latter Day Saints. My area of assignment was the New Zealand Auckland area and there I spent a year in and around Auckland and a year in the Cook Islands. Again, I learned invaluable lessons on service and selflessness while serving the people of the islands, too many to cover in this writing. By the time my twenty-four months were up, I was again gainfully unemployed and looking for a regular paycheck.

Since my youth I had always wanted to be a policeman. I had actually applied straight out of school (before my trolley boy days) but was rejected on account of my asthma. Now I felt I had much more to offer the force, considering my employment and service experience, and was accepted into the Queensland Police Academy in December 1989. It was a great month, as I had also asked Caroline Fulcher for her hand in marriage. She also accepted.

The next twelve years were some of the most enjoyable times in my occupational life. The attributes of a great police officer seemed to be a combination of what I had learned in my previous two assignments:

1. Connecting with people
2. A willingness to serve others

I loved the visibility of being in uniform and the ability to serve individuals in the community. Yes, there were the unpleasant tasks as well, but in the end, the positive experiences always outweighed the negative. The benefits and security were also good. Working for the government meant job stability and security. When people asked how the police work was going I was always replied, "Great—we're getting new customers every day!" There was also a structured paycheck with the ability of regular overtime, which worked well for us bringing up a young family.

Coming into the year 2000, we had some interesting opportunities and choices to make. Policing was becoming increasingly hazardous with the advent of needled drugs and the danger of needle stick injuries, of which I was a recipient. After a round of monthly blood tests to confirm I hadn't contracted Hepatitis C, the shine of policing was losing its lustre and I was open to other opportunities. I was the officer in charge of a small police station at the time, and advancement in the department either meant going back out on the road on twenty-four-hourly shifts or sitting at a desk. I didn't have a passion for either.

At about this time a good friend had asked me at a family BBQ whether we would be interested in going into the Frozen Custard business. "What the blazes is Frozen Custard?" It was barely heard of in Brisbane, Australia.

After a quick trip to the United States touring the famous and not so famous ice cream and frozen custard stores of Wisconsin and consuming a copious amount of ice cream, we set about weighing up the pros and cons of leaving a secure government job and going into the uncertain world of private enterprise.

The police scene was getting a little stressful, not to mention much more violent than when I had first joined over a decade earlier. I thought I would have much less stress running an ice cream business—yeah right! I soon learned that running an ice cream business and eating ice cream were two entirely different things. In fact sometimes I would rather be dragging a 6'4" drunk out of a dingy Irish tavern late on a Friday Night than having to stay up and do inventory again.

In fact the only principle the two occupations had in common was that I had to put a rubber glove on for both jobs. However my policing customers were never as excited to see me snap on the latex as the ice cream customers were.

This was also an entirely different mindset for me occupationally. I was used to being a government employee, with an "eight hours work for eight hours pay" mentality. If I worked one minute over my assigned shift, I qualified for double time and a half. This is what I thought all employment was like.

Some days in the ice cream shop, I was working more than fourteen hours a day with no "overtime clock" ticking. I must admit—it was a difficult adjustment to make.

Our team went through the process of designing and getting the store built out, ordering and installing equipment, hiring and training staff, and finally getting the store ready to open. It was a bumpy start but we felt we had achieved a great deal with little to no foodservice experience. After six weeks or so, when we felt we were ready, we decided to have a grand opening fit for a king. We wanted to let the world know who we were and why they should come and buy the best ice cream in town from us. We spent a generous amount of money on radio advertising, organized a large inflatable dome to be erected in the parking lot, ice cream eating competitions, clowns, face painting, the whole shebang.

My wife Caroline was chief face painter and costume designer. She sewed a beautiful pair of baggy silk clown pants, suspenders and all. The trousers were accompanied with a wide spotted silk tie, oversized shoes, an orange lapel flower and a bright green wig. It was an outfit that Ronald would have been proud of.

As the big day drew closer, and all of our responsibilities and stresses grew, I assumed that someone would put their hand up to volunteer for the position of Chief Promotions Officer (Clown suit wearer). After all, I was far too important to dilly dally around in a bozo outfit. It goes to show—you should never assume.

The morning of our grand opening, amidst the hustle and bustle of staff members, face painters and legitimate clowns on unicycles, the $64 question was asked, *"Who's going to wear the green wig? Someone's got to wear the green wig!"* Well, needless to say, you don't get the $64 for guessing who spent the rest of the day as BoBo. Yours truly.

And I don't mind saying, fifteen years down the road, I still have that wig and baggy trousers and I wear them regularly (in a professional sense that is).

The Author and daughters Emily, Lizzie & Maddie

We opened another location, added a food truck to our offering, and ran those businesses through the highs and lows for a number of years. In 2004, the company that we purchased our specialty ice cream equipment from offered me a job to move to the United States and help grow their business. Thus we start our adventure into the world of ice cream and frozen dessert consultancy and education.

Now granted my particular experience is in ice cream and frozen desserts. One important note is that the principles in this book stretch over the broad spectrum of small business customer service scenarios. From hot dogs to hardware, from dance classes to dandelions—the principles of finding, training and motivating super employees are basically the same.

I trust you will enjoy this work and draw some benefit from these pages to apply to your own business success.

ii. Introduction

Warning—Self-promotion alert. I have had the great opportunity to develop a reputation in the foodservice realm as an industry expert. I have consulted with international food chains, quick service restaurants, resort complexes and casinos. I have trained and toiled in the kitchens of national brand restaurants, resorts and hundreds of franchised and independently owned businesses alike. On numerous occasions, I have been permitted into the secret test kitchens of international brands and food concepts known worldwide to develop recipes, programs and processes.

My industry knowledge and the ability to convey that knowledge effectively (with a little comedy routine thrown in) has resulted in invitations to present keynote addresses, workshops, presentations and speeches in universities, trade shows, conventions and restaurant industry events all over the world.

I have trained literally tens of thousands in retail management, marketing and promotion, menu development and customer service techniques. Now granted my expertise is centered on the development of ice cream and frozen dessert businesses, however regardless of the particular concept, most of the challenges in retail businesses are similar.

In all of this experience in the retail food and service industry, do you know the most common questions I am asked by business owners across the retail and wholesale landscape?

How do I get my employees to care?

How do I engage my employees so they don't just work hard when I am there?

How do I raise the minimum standard of work performance from mediocre to magnificence?

The Survey Says…

Prior to going to press, I sent out a survey to over seven thousand individuals who operate, manage or are in the process of starting up their own retail or wholesale business. The final question of the survey was as follows:

What is the most important issue you are dealing with when it comes to your employees?

The results were an overwhelming confirmation that many small business owners, both retail and wholesale, in the food, product or service industry, struggle with the same issues when it comes to dealing with employees. Some of the most common responses were centered on these concerns:

"Accountability — no one seems to care about anything other than themselves."

"Do they fully understand the importance of customer service?"

"Lack of Commitment!"

"Buying in to wanting to do a good job; having them understand that they represent me as much as I represent them. Having them

understand that the goal is to make money and it takes a total team effort."

"Instilling a sense of value in their minds; some have good value systems coming in, but some don't and those are the ones that it takes quite a bit to build up."

"The last thing I want my employees to think is that they must show up to just do a job—a job that they dread for whatever reason. They must feel like they are a needed component. They must feel a strong sense of belonging."

"Improve their sense of responsibility, their customer interaction skills, and their understanding that rules and policies are there for a purpose."

"Willingness to work, stay motivated and get the job done right the first time. A better understanding of how business operates."

"I want them to care about the business."

I am almost positive that many of you reading these comments can relate to the exact wording of some of statements. I know I have felt each one of these concerns at some stage during my operational experiences.

These are the questions and the issues that face the nation. If small business is the backbone of this and most other countries, and employees primarily run small business, there is a direct correlation between small business employees and the success of business as a whole.

Taking your employees from "Hopeless to Hero" status starts all the way back in the thought process of how you want your business to be run. It involves where you source your employees from, what your application looks like and how you orientate them. I am supremely confident this book will give you a leg up in getting the most out of your hired help.

Three Key Elements to Retail Business Success.
I believe there are three key elements to success in any retail business. I call them the three "En's"

1. End Product
2. Environment
3. Engagement

Most businesses focus on their end product or service as a key indicator of retail success. They are under the mistaken belief that if the product or service that the customer is purchasing is of a higher quality or standard than their competition, that will lead to increased business.

Let me tell you that I've visited many businesses that had great end products but still eventually went out of business. Though the quality of your end product is *one* of the key elements, it is not the only key indicator of business success.

The second element of success is the *environment* in which this product or service is provided. Having any fun and entertaining environment only adds to the entire retail experience. Let me give you an example.

We opened an ice cream store in St Louis Missouri called Mr. C's Ice Cream Emporium. Many of our customers noted that we were only a stone's throw away from many other ice cream or frozen dessert locations. When competition is close by, it is very hard to go up against them based on product alone. Families and individuals do not go from restaurant to restaurant, or ice cream store to ice cream store, sampling food to determine who has the better products.

What *is* important to many potential customers is the environment in which they're going to enjoy their product or service. In fact most customers attending a new restaurant or retail store will take in their surroundings and make a judgment on what the product will be like simply based on the way the premises is presented to them.

Interior and exterior décor and layout can be huge factors as to whether potential customers will stop and stay in your place of business. Let me give you an example.

From the Cows to the Cone

I often visit a burger and frozen custard chain in Milwaukee named Kopp's Frozen Custard. On my very first visit, before I even got into the store, I noticed a long line of Cow statues lining the rear of the parking lot. Customers were taking photographs of kids draped all over these bovines, despite the signs asking customers to stay off the cows. Before people were even walking inside the building, they were already having an engaging experience. I decided right then and there that I wanted my store to have at least one cow.

When the time for layout, design and build out came for our location in St Louis, I had already purchased a cow from an online store, in none other than Texas. Where else would you buy a cow?

In fact I got lucky and picked up a calf for half price at the same time.

I have seen over the years many customers point up to the cows on the mezzanine, showing their kids or relatives our two mascots, Matilda and Clarence. I have overheard kids in the local grocery store asking Mom to take them to the "Cow Ice Cream Store." Let me tell you from personal and professional experience— environment matters!

Engagement Is the Key

Despite your best efforts in the design and layout of your business, or the quality and value of your product, you can still have an extremely flat atmosphere without the right staff to represent your business and to serve your customers' needs. I keep saying time and time again:

"You are not just in the food business; you are in the entertainment business."

Customers need to feel engaged, appreciated and wanted. It simply isn't enough to keep your customers satisfied anymore. Customers need to be engaged and excited about your business to keep coming back. *End Product, Environment* and *Engagement* are the three key elements to keep your customers coming back, to keep them entertained. In order to succeed here, the right person to engage and exceed your customers' needs is essential.

I was working at a trade show in Houston Texas, whereby the third day of the show, things were getting a little monotonous in the booth. It was a quiet day and the flow of prospects and passersby was steadily thinning. The fact that we were giving away a premium ice cream product still didn't seem to draw much of a crowd. Our booth was professionally designed and laid out. Our backdrop was impressive and our machinery was gleaming, yet there seemed to be no atmosphere, no electricity in the booth. We had an excellent end product and our environment was professional and eye catching.

It seemed our only steady stream of visitors came with their "Hot Spot Competition form." Prior to the commencement of the show, our company had signed up to participate in a competition where customers could win a large screen television. All they had to do was find a large "Hot Spot" sign located at several booths around the convention hall and get a stamp in the appropriate place on their game card. Once the card was full, it was handed in and placed in the draw for the television. Well, some of these budding winners were downright rude, pushing their game card in our faces without some much as a "How's your father?"

It was under these circumstances that a seemingly great idea was born. We decided that we were no longer going to give these stamps out for free. These people wanting something for nothing were now going to have to *work* for the privilege of a winning stamp. They were now going to have to play and win "Musical Trivia." We came up with several songs from the 70s, 80s, 90s and current top forty hits. We would sing the first few bars and they would have to sing the next line.

Our first customer approached with paper in hand. *"I'm sorry, Madam, but in order to get a stamp you have to play musical trivia."* A puzzled look came across her face.

"What era would you like to play from, 70s, 80s, 90s or current top forty hits?" *"Ahh, 80s I guess,"* she stammered.

I turned to our hastily prepared contest sheet and started to sing...
"On a dark desert highway, cool wind in my hair, warm smell of colitas..."
"Oh...um..."
A huge grin spread across her face. *"Rising up from the air?"*
"Yes!" I shouted, *"We have a winner."*

She had conquered, received her well-earned stamp and walked away bemused. We continued the play the game, one contestant after another until, in a matter of fifteen minutes or so, we had about thirty or forty people crowded around our booth.

Some were there legitimately to compete for a stamp. The others were with the contestants helping them with answers. Staff from neighboring booths had also come over, and before you knew it, we were working the crowd and having a great time. The atmosphere was fun and electric, and I am sure most people there walked away from the area thinking they had just had some serious fun.

That's the impression you want from people who leave your business. You want them to remember the experience they had in your part of the world for the short time they were there. Having exciting and enthusiastic employees is a key element in providing that experience.

This is the core message in this book. From the time you start your search for new employees, all the way through to your ongoing customer service training efforts, there are elements and steps to have in place so your employees can care as much about your business as you do. To have new employees who excel and to morph your current employees from hopeless to hero status.

Chapter 1 The Pimple-Faced Sixteen-Year-Old Kid

I, like most of you, have been on many ends of the retail business. I have obviously been a customer at many establishments over the years and have formed an opinion as to what the customer service standard should be—*as a customer*. I have a set of standards in my mind as to what an acceptable level of customer service is in most situations, as do you.

I have also been an employer—the one responsible for hiring and firing retail employees. At one stage we had a total of about forty employees who I was responsible for. I interviewed, hired and trained them. I also let a few go in my time for a variety of reasons. It's not the most pleasant experience, particularly the first time, but believe me, its gets easier over time.

I have worked for a manufacturer where equipment was designed and engineered, manufactured and sold through a distribution network. Each piece of equipment was made to order and tested before going out into the field. I have worked trade show booths all around the world representing and demonstrating this equipment.

I have interacted with employers and employees as a trainer and facilitator in workshops ranging in number from three to three hundred. These workshops and training sessions have been conducted all through the United States, Australia and through Europe.

In every one of these scenarios, the same quintessential person rears his ugly head. His reputation goes before him. He is both loved and feared by all industries. His name is held for good and evil everywhere it is mentioned. He is:

The pimply-faced sixteen-year-old kid.

Most business owners and employers in the retail food or service business know what I am talking about. Most retail food equipment manufacturers, sales and marketing people know this guy as well. Potential business owners, who have yet to dip their big toe in the pool of business ownership, know this guy—and they have never even met him.

He is like the Kaiser Sousse of employees. He is everywhere, and yet—he is nowhere. He is the lowest common denominator in any workplace and yet is the backbone of small business. If a system or procedure is being put into place, it needs to be tailored toward the *pimply-faced sixteen-year-old kid.* Workplace policies and procedures must have a comprehension standard at this guy's level. His needs, wants, and abilities are factored into every level of policy, procedure, design and manufacturing.

Food equipment manufacturers and processors design and build their equipment at his level. He is ... *The pimply-faced sixteen-year-old kid.*

Personally, I think the pimply-faced sixteen-year-old kid gets a bad rap. Perhaps there was a bad batch of pimply-faced sixteen-year-old kids at one stage and all of them since are painted with the same tarnished brush. I myself have met many nice pimply-faced sixteen-year-old kids. I think I may have been one of them once. Regardless of your personal opinion, this is a very real perception in the retail product and service business that employs persons from age sixteen years and up. He is feared all over the world.

The question that faces the nation is—how do you get this kid, and the other demographically equivalent employees like him, to really care about their jobs? And not just care, but excel at their job. Well there is a formula and that's what this book is all about. From the application, to the audition, through the training, opening and ongoing education, we can rebuild him. We have the technology.

From Dance Parties to Employee of the Month
So we had this urban rapper as an employee at one of our stores—cap on a tilt, pants hanging low and a swagger that would make the Biebs proud (more on the hanging pants later). He was very confident and engaging but not always reliable. One Saturday afternoon, after I had finished some yard work at our home, I had bundled up some leaf bags to take to the store. Having your own personal dumpster is one of the greatest perks of business ownership.

As I pulled around the back of our ice cream store, I came across an impromptu dance party in full swing. Our urban rapper had pulled his car up to the back of the store, opened the doors and cranked up a sweet beat. Then he sent out a Facebook invitation to his friends to come by the store to "drop it like it's hot" for an hour or so.

By the time I pulled around the corner, there were seven or eight youths either sitting on the wall with heads bobbing up and down to the beat or trying out some new sick dance moves. In one fluid motion, I swung around to the epicenter of the rave, wound down my driver's window and in a fit of rage yelled out, "What the Hell is going on here?"

You should have seen those kids scatter like cockroaches. I was too angry to even talk to the two employees who should have been inside the store working on their task list and prepping for the night's business. Even when an apology was attempted, I put my hand up and stated, *"Don't talk to me just now. I am still very angry!"* I did have a heart to heart with them individually to convey my disappointment in their behavior, at a later time.

Fast forward a couple of months, and another incident with our urban rapper. Again, I was almost brought to tears over his actions, however this time they were tears of joy. I came into the store to check on things. Those of you who have a retail store or business know that this is a task that is repeated over and over. For no particular reason, it is very beneficial to drop in unexpectedly. Keeps the natives on their toes so to speak. Here is our own personal Ludacris standing out in the customer area. No, he wasn't rapping or busting a move. He was bending over and helping an elderly customer read the menu and pointing out the particular menu items that he felt she would be interested in.

I stood in the doorway—silent. I listened and learned as he very respectfully, and somewhat tenderly, helped our guest select an item that would be in her price range and would satisfy her need for a treat. It wasn't till he had helped her make the decision and came back around to the register side of the counter that he noticed me.
I gave him the thumbs up, wiped away a little tear from my cheek, and after she left, took some time to congratulate him on his actions. He had just earned our "Employee of the Month" award.

More on that later. The point of the story is that every employee, regardless of their background, circumstances or personality, can be molded into an exceptional employee and become a very real asset to your business.

Are They Really Hopeless?

When I sent a survey out prior to this book's release, I included the title "From Hopeless to Hero" in the post. A dear family friend from Australia took umbrage at the title and gently reminded me that "no one is really hopeless." She brings up a great point.

Those of us who work in the retail food or other service related industries can sometimes feel as though the reality of getting outstanding, or "super employees" is just a pipe dream and the vision of having their crew really care about their businesses is a hopeless one. Some just flat out think there is no hope to help their employees rise up over a mediocre level of passion and work ethic. That's what this book is all about. It's the good news of retail employees! There is hope.

I firmly believe that following the principles and processes in this book will help you make heroes out of the seemingly hopeless. Think about the restaurants and cafes you have eaten in regularly. I want you to think about the quality of customer service and attention you were given. Does poor customer service make up for good tasting food? Generally not. Most people would not return to a restaurant where the service was poor no matter how good the food tasted.

Now on the flip side of that—does excellent and attentive customer service make up for average food? Of course it does.

A great percentage of the restaurants in the US have average food, however the Americans know how to do one thing very well—customer service. That's what makes restaurants who sell average food do very well. These "hole in the wall" burger, fast food, and dessert places are some of the most popular, best kept secrets of the industry.

And the core of customer service is the person you select to deliver it to the customer—the employee.

Chapter 2   A Horror Story

I tell you this story very early on in this piece not to scare you or turn you off the whole process of finding and training good employees altogether.

I tell you this story because there are many facets to finding and training super employees. This won't be a quick process for you, although once finished putting all of the essential elements in place, it can be maintained more efficiently than the first time you go through the process. I also tell you this story to illustrate the ramifications of shooting from the hip and making a "quick hire" because it's convenient, rather than taking the time and effort to really investigate your potential new employees.

So settle in, grab a pillow to periodically hide your eyes and... read on! Oh and by the way, names have been changed to protect the incompetent.

One of our ice cream stores had been open about three and a half years. We were winding down from our summer season and had lost some of our key shift managers as they left to return to college. We found ourselves having to make a decision to hire a manager as quickly as we could. My general manager Andrea had mentioned that she had worked previously with a friend of hers in a food establishment and felt that she may be a good hire for us.

Andrea said that her friend was currently looking for work and thought she would be a good fit into our establishment. I reiterated to her, as I do with all of my employees, that in making a recommendation of a friend, family member or associate, their reputation is on the line as well. Andrea put her reputation on the line and said that she would interview her. Then comes the proverbial fork in the road.

Before I tell you what I said next, I have utilized the principle of hindsight to acknowledge that this statement should never have been said. It was a moment of weakness on my part due to the fact that I thought this may be an "easy fix" to an employment problem. I had a million and a half tasks to do and it is always at this time that we try and take a shortcut.

I said, and I quote, *"I will interview her but barring she stabs me in the interview, I think we could give her the job."*

I should have NEVER said that. Whenever you give anyone an indication that they will have the job without giving yourself time to reflect after the interview, you are in no man's land or backed up against the wall. The time of the interview had arrived and I pulled up to the store to see my potential new hire. Now again I am exposing another character flaw here.

Before I continue with the story, let me segue here by saying that in the customer service industry, we don't necessarily look for supermodels. A person's looks generally do not have bearing on how hard they are going to work or how punctual they may be. That being said, employees who represent your business, particularly those who are serving customers, should be well presented, neat and tidy. Before any of your potential customers taste any of your products or experience any of your service, they are making a determination as to what your product or service is like based on the appearance of the person standing in front of them. It sounds pretty corny but you never get a second chance at a first impression. We have had employees of all different shapes and sizes work for us over the years. My only stipulation was that they were clean, neat, tidy and wearing a pressed uniform at the beginning of every shift. I don't think that's too much to ask in my humble opinion.

That being said let's go back to the story.

I could see Danielle sitting in the booth from where I was parked in the parking lot, and simply stated, she certainly did not fit the usual demographic of most of our other employees.

The second thing I noticed was that she was wearing white trousers. This was important because not many people wear white trousers, however our uniform requirement was, you guessed it.. white trousers. She had obviously tracked them down and purchased them because in her mind she knew that if she got through this interview without stabbing me, she would have the job. And why wouldn't she? *That's what I said.*

I walked in, offered my greetings to everybody, and sat down in the booth opposite her. She greeted me with a very gravelly voice. It was either a very bad godfather impression or the result of many years of chain-smoking. The yellow stains on her fingers and nails led me to believe the latter.

And yet I wasn't in the market for a beauty queen or an opera singer; I needed someone who could adequately manage a shift in my ice cream store. We went through the questions and she gave me textbook answers. I had no choice but to congratulate her on the job with a less than the heartfelt handshake. In my heart I knew that this was not my ideal employee, but I felt trapped into hiring her. As the younger employees filtered in for the evening shift, they pointed at her and gave me an inquisitive look. As if to say, "What's this all about?"

"Leave me alone and get back to work," I muttered.

It was only two weeks before the complaints started rolling in. Some employees complained that Danielle was taking longer than her requisite thirty-minute meal break—some nights much longer.

I spoke to her and the other shift managers, telling them they were on an hourly wage and if they needed to go and attend to family matters or "other than work" responsibilities, they needed to check out of the register before they took extended breaks. Everyone agreed that they would comply as well as old "gravel throat" at the back of the room.

Next, a collection of cigarette butts started to grow at the back door of the store. If there's one thing I cannot stand it is employees of any business standing at the back of the store smoking. Our GM Andrea had been a smoker for years but she was what I call a "phantom smoker." I never smelled smoke on her breath or her clothes and there was never any indication that she had smoked at all.

I knew only too well whose cigarette butts they were. I had *another* meeting explaining that we do not smoke on or near the premises particularly at the back door. Employees could smoke in their cars if they really felt the need during the workday. It got to the point that whenever I would drive past the store, I would check to see whose car was in the parking lot. If Danielle was running the shift I would just continue on rather than stopping in and see how things were going. Isn't that ridiculous?

That I would put myself in a situation where I wouldn't even go to my own ice cream store so as not to talk or have to engage with one of my employees. I think back to that pivotal moment and wished that I had taken another, less convenient route.

The final straw came when another of our shift managers, Brian, asked to talk to me about one of our employees. I let out a heavy sigh. I knew who it would be. Brian said that a couple of days ago he went to the freezer to get frozen cookie pucks out in order to make ice cream sandwiches. We had a small oven in the store that we would bake the frozen dough and then assemble the sandwich treats.

However when he went to the box, there were only two or three frozen pieces left from the thirty or forty there were the day before. The cupboard was bare. When he asked Danielle what happened to the cookies, she said that she had taken them home to bake for her son's school lunches. As if that wasn't bad enough she also admitted, quite proudly, that she had taken a bag of peanut butter cups as well.

I was instantly angry. All of the other bits and pieces of her bad behavior paled to insignificance compared to what I was hearing.

Just when I thought it couldn't get any worse, Brian dropped another clanger. Apparently after this conversation, he was signing out of the register to end his shift, and she said to him, and I quote,

"Don't sign out just yet—you go home and I will sign you out in an hour or so, you can get a little more money that way."

If I hadn't reached my limit until then, it just boiled over. Now I have always told my employees that if they see anything happening in the workplace that they feel is dishonest or just plain wrong, I will never drop their name as an informant. Yes, our "whistle blowing protection program" was in full effect. In this particular case, I breached protocol. I was dialing her number before Brian even finished his sentence and before long, that gravelly voice was answering the phone.

"Danielle, Brian tells me you took a boxful of cookies and a bag of peanut butter cups home for your kids?"

Without hesitation she growled back a comment that my ten-year-old son would probably say in the same situation.

"You can come over and search my house, I don't have them."

Now I said something next that I am not very proud of here and I wouldn't usually confess to such behavior, but it paints a picture as to how angry and frustrated I was.

I said, *"Oh I know you don't have them there now—I don't think they even made it past the drive home."* (I still feel a little bad about that one). I continued, *"I don't want to see you back in the store ever again. We are winding down for the season and are reducing shifts, so please hand your uniform to Angie so she can bring it in."* Then I hung up.

Now...I want to take you back, in a fast rewind, back to the fork in the road at the beginning of the story. Standing at that fork in the road there with Andrea suggesting her friend as a potential employee should have gone thus:

I should have said, *"Well that's a great option, but I think we need to have a few options. Options are good. Let's ask the existing staff if they have any recommendations and go through our previous applications and get a group of five or so applicants. If Danielle is the right person for the job, we can offer her some work."*

I will guarantee that if you attend any business, restaurant or service-oriented trade show or convention anywhere in the country, you will hear horror stories like this (and worse) from nearly every small business owner you talk to. I have often said, and still say, "If I could get rid of all my employees, and if I could get rid of all my customers, I would love to go to work in my business every day."

This would ring true if customers and employees didn't directly relate to your revenue, income and overall business success.

Your employees are the core of your business. Your employees are *you* when you are not there to personally greet, serve and thank your customers. Your employees are the difference between good revenue and great revenue. Just as you research and study the features and benefits of an expensive piece of equipment before you invest in purchasing it, so you should research the features and benefits of your potential employees before hiring them.

Let me tell you that there is no shortcut or fast track to having super employees. I already knew that at the time, but the pulls of time constraints, "busyness" and other tasks pulling you away from this important process, will have you thinking that you can bypass the tried and true processes we will discuss in this book.

Don't succumb to this pattern of thought. You will have many other seemingly important tasks to perform and things to do and making a "convenient" decision on a quick hire will ultimately cost you more time, effort and money that you ever would have imagined.

Chapter 3   Know the Law

In this chapter we are going to talk a little bit about your rights and responsibilities as an employer and what you should know about the labor laws in your particular area. Before you look at the first application or formulate your training program, you must have a good understanding as to the rights and responsibilities you and your employees have in the workplace.

Let me start by saying that this topic is certainly not the fun stuff about running your business, however these are principles of the law that you do not want to simply gloss over. Labor Department fines are some of the largest in existence, so knowing your rights and also the rights of your employees is essential as a business owner and may save you a small fortune.

State and Federal Law

As with other areas of small business, the federal government and the state government will more than likely have legislation that applies to your process of hiring and maintaining a group of employees. As a general rule of thumb, the federal government maintains a standard that is applicable all over the entire country and its territories.

The only time you would not adhere to the federal law is if a state determines the federal law is not strong enough, stringent enough or applicable in certain situations. The state has the right to rewrite and submit to the legislature, statutes that are more applicable or stringent in their particular area of responsibility.

An example would be where the federal law mandates a certain requirement or standard for employing youth or elderly folk. Some states that have an inordinate amount of elderly, such as Florida, might determine that some of the legislation is not stringent enough to cover their older working population. This being the case, they would write into the law requirements that would be more stringent to protect the individual's rights. These statutes would then supersede the federal law.

Generally the federal law is the standard, but most states have their own legislation that uses the federal law as the base and then creates more applicable content in relation to their particular population and work force. Contacting your state labor office will generally point you in the right direction.

Get It from the Horse's Mouth.
Numerous stories have been related to me where the owner of a small business recently purchased the business from the previous owner. This previous owner offered to stay on for two to four weeks and help with the general running an education process of the business.

This works well for general policy and procedure but when you are taking advice, particularly in relation to Health, Building or Labor Department policy from a store owner who may be using legislation that is out of date, you may find yourself in real hot water.

One particular new business owner was applying the principles and practices told to him by the previous owner and was doing so outside the boundary of the labor laws of his particular state. When a complaint was made and the Labor Department investigated, it was found that the information this new business owner received from the previous owner was out of date and now this new business owner found himself outside the law.

The exact amount was not told to me but the fine was in the tens of thousands of dollars. As mentioned Labor Department fines can be the largest you will come across in the process of running your business so taking the time and effort to get the points of law from either a representative of the state labor department or from their website is very, very important.

Regardless of where you are in the process of your business, whether a seasoned veteran or a relative newbie, take the time to make contact with your relevant Labor Department representative.

Think you know generally what your state labor regulations are? Think again. This legislation can change from state to state and can contain some complex and detailed information that you need to be aware of as an employer. Some examples of topics you may find in your state labor law that apply to your business are as follows:

- ✓ Hours of work restrictions for employing minors
- ✓ School and study requirements for student employees
- ✓ Equipment operation restrictions
- ✓ Requirements for forms and certificates needed
- ✓ Disability Act regulations and requirements
- ✓ Discrimination guidelines and statutes
- ✓ Equal Pay Act regulations and requirements
- ✓ Employer Tax Code and regulations
- ✓ Prevailing minimum wage guidelines
- ✓ Labor relations and Union responsibilities

- ✓ Arbitration information for employees
- ✓ Occupational health and safety requirements
- ✓ Unemployment classifications and rights
- ✓ Workers Compensation regulations
- ✓ Discipline and termination rules and regulations
- ✓ Immigrants and authorized alien worker permits
- ✓ Insurance required in the workplace
- ✓ Vacation and sick day regulations
- ✓ Drug and alcohol regulations
- ✓ Requirements for chemicals and solvents in the workplace
- ✓ Penalties for violations

So as you glance over this reduced list of topics that are probably in your state labor regulations, hopefully it will stir some feelings within you that there is a lot to be aware of. This doesn't even count the irregular topics such as inventions made by employees and lactation rights. Do yourself a favor and familiarize yourself with these topics. They make for great late night reading.

Illegal and Legal Discrimination

While covering state mandated law, let me talk here a little about discrimination. Discrimination has become such a negative word particularly when it's used in relation to the employment or hiring process. But let's face it we use the principles of discrimination every day. When I am standing in a McDonald's I am discriminating against every other burger when I choose a quarter pounder with cheese. While I'm getting dressed for church on Sunday, I discriminate against three hundred other ties when I choose my pink polka dot tie.

When I take my wife out for a date at the movies, I discriminate against fifteen other titles by choosing a particular movie to see. We discriminate every day. Discrimination is a wonderful principle. Discrimination means we have choice and the freedom to choose among those choices. We typically use discrimination to make good choices which in turn have positive consequences and outcomes.

Yes granted that sometimes we make wrong choices and the following consequences may not be the best, but this is one of the greatest principles we enjoy in life. Having our choice or the ability to discriminate taken away from us robs us of our God-given right to use our conscience and previous experience to choose wisely and benefit from those choices.

Now I unequivocally support illegal discrimination in the hiring process. Every applicant deserves the right to be considered on merits and not by gender or skin color or religious preference or any of the other state mandated elements of the law. But let's get down to tin tacks here. On some occasions, you are sifting through fifty applications for a particular job at your business. You are not looking for fifty positions to fill. Let's say you have ten positions or even five that you need to fill.

Regardless how you go through the decision-making process, you are about to discriminate against forty-five people in order to get the best five applicants. This form of discrimination is a good thing. It is the same process of purchasing a piece of equipment for your business. You weigh the pros and cons of each option and make a decision that best suits you.

The employment application process is the same; the difference is you are going through the process of weighing up the pros and cons of each applicant. You will look at their personalities, their appearances, their previous experiences as well as many other factors to determine whether each person is a good fit for your business.

When you go through this process, remember that this person will be standing at the register representing not only your product or service but you personally. No one will ever be appreciative of or welcome your customers like you do, but you can't be everywhere doing everything.

So the next best thing is to select employees who closely align with your business and customer service ethos. So in essence, don't feel as though you need to hire someone just because you are afraid they may be offended or feel as though you are discriminating against them. The simple fact of the matter is you did discriminate against them.

You chose someone else who had better qualifications and better "chops" for the job. Now again just to reiterate that state or federal mandated discrimination policies must always be adhered to and if you are not aware of your legal obligations when it comes to discrimination, you will need to get educated. The line can get a little fuzzy at times.

Take tattoos for example. To my knowledge there is no state or federal legislation that says that you must employ someone who has visible tattoos. Tattoos don't happen by accident. You aren't born with tattoos. Yes admittedly there probably have been many tattoos that have been discovered after a heavy night of drinking where permission to the tattoo artist has been loosely given through slurred speech.

That being the case, tattoos are a choice that a person makes. I'm sure they went through the process of discrimination to choose which particular pattern or image they wanted tattooed on their body. *"Should I get the goat's head or the love heart with Mom"*

If I am running a family oriented business, let's say for example an ice cream store, I am quite within my rights to not employ somebody because they have visible tattoos. This is my right as an employer. Regardless of their previous experience qualifications or personality, if I don't feel their appearance is a match for my business I am quite within my rights to not offer them a job. This area comes under your own policy and procedure regulations such as "Grooming and Dress Requirements."

Or I may offer them a position so long as they can cover the tattoo if possible. I once saw one of my managers come into the store in her spare time and noticed a tattoo on her wrist. She had been working for me for about two years and I commented on it as I thought it had been recently acquired.

She told me she had got it many years ago but she chooses to wear a sweat band over the image so as to not "put people off" in her words. It was only then that I remembered she wore a sweatband on her wrist to work every day.

The opposite of this story is an experience I had with a young man I was once interviewing. I was constantly distracted by the gauze patch on his head and before long I couldn't help myself. I asked him if he had bumped or scratched himself. He replied that he had given himself a tattoo recently and asked if I would like to see it.

"Most certainly," I said.

He carefully peeled back the gauze pad to reveal the word "H E L P" written backwards on his forehead (unfortunately I couldn't find a font to reflect the actual appearance of the letters). It was right about that time I made my decision not to hire him. He lost me at "H."

Take the recent grumblings in the state of Colorado as another example. The passing in legislation to make marijuana legal under certain considerations has caused a slew of complaints and lawsuits by employees fired because of their marijuana use. Some users may claim that because the law now permits the use of pot, it is discriminatory to fire an employee because of his usage. Here is where the line needs to be drawn as to what is *legal* and what is *acceptable* under your business' policy. Alcohol consumption has been legal for decades and yet improper consumption or showing up to work hung-over, or even worse, intoxicated, can still get you fired, no matter how legal it is to consume liquor.

There can be some common ground in relation to these principles. A young man came to interview for a job and had a large diamond stud in his ear (although I suspect it was a cubic zirconia). Our policy was that the girls could have no dangling earrings and there were to be no earrings or studs for our male employees.

Regardless of what you think of me or how antiquated my thought process is, this is my preference. I told the young man that we could possibly have some work for him as long as he was comfortable enough not to wear the stud during work hours.

He looked at me very strangely as if I had been thrust forward from the 1800s. Regardless of what he thought, that was my principle—my rule. He accepted the job and removed the said earpiece during his scheduled shifts. We should all be celebrating the right we have to make these choices.

Chapter 4   Where Do I find Great Employees?

The ways to get the word out that you are hiring are many and varied, and some have higher rates of success than others.

Believe me when I tell you that you should only have to do this once. Once you have a good solid core of dependable and hardworking employees, you should be drawing from their peer group or family members for further potential staff members. If Amber is an A Grade student, plays an instrument and has a great positive mental attitude, you can bet your bottom dollar she is not hanging around with the local crack heads. People tend to befriend people their own likes, standards and values.

When a position looks like it will come available within a couple of weeks, ask Amber if she has any friends or family who may be interested in a position at your store. The only scenario where this wouldn't work is if the actual person the friend was going to replace was Amber herself. That wouldn't be very good.

That being said, every now and then you will need to go fishing for new employees. Every good fisherman (and my family is full of them) knows the secret and special spots to pull in the big one. Here are some examples.

Fish in the Right Pools
Words of warning here before you make any rash decisions or click the send button for that online classified website. Take a breath and ask yourself, "Do you know what you're getting yourself into?"

What is going to be the impending result, when and where you post this request for hire? Are you simply baiting and throwing a hook out there in the easiest and biggest pool of fish that contains every kind of fish both good and bad.

Remember Mullet and Mahi Mahi swim in the same water.

You want to save yourself time and money here by not pulling in any old fish. The time taken to reel it in, have a good look to gauge its size, unhook and throw it back in is too valuable to waste. Doing it right the first time will save you a world of hurt. You need to concentrate your efforts and fish in the right pools.

Social or Classified Websites

There are many websites that are classified or socially based that attract a lot of people. You can buy cars or used furniture. You can chat about the weather or how the Cardinals are doing this season. You can even browse the casual encounters looking for love. I put it to you that this is not the kind of source you want to be pulling your applicants from. The talent in this pool typically hangs around the shallow end. If an online site has a core focus on employment and developing employment skills, that is another thing.

I have said a hundred times in class that if the same people who are looking for applications to work in your business are mingling with other online visitors who are looking for prostitutes to kill, that is not the kind of guy I want representing my business.

High School, College and University Websites and Forums

These avenues of gaining employees can be very effective. Remember that you will more than likely get a lot of bites here;

make sure your filtering process is fine-tuned. College applicants are great shift managers or supervisors and are generally motivated by the need for cash.

You can also acquire some great and evolving talent to develop others areas of your business. Hiring a marketing major as a shift manager can have a dual purpose as you utilize your field of study to grow your influence in the social media realm. Having an accounting student on the books can give him or her real world business management experience and free up some of your admin time to concentrate on growing your business.

My daughter Elizabeth found a posting on her university's website and applied for an internship as a marketing and business manager for a local ice cream chain based out of her college town. Within weeks she was managing several locations and also working in the corporate office assisting with training and employees and fine-tuning operations at several of the chains locations.

Similarly high school employment programs can help do some filtering for you. One word of caution—spread the concentration of high school students where you can. I try to draw from several high schools within the geographic radius of my businesses. This way if a major school sporting event or dance is coming up, you don't lose all of your employees for a crucial Friday night's trade.

Retiree Associations
This can be a real fruit salad when it comes to your potential applicants from retirees associations. Some would say that these are people with a lot of life experience and wisdom under their hat and they would probably be correct.

Having a retired marketing or business manager working in your business could boost your knowledge base significantly. One new ice cream business owner employed an older gent who had spent twenty years making ice cream cakes for Baskin Robbins. This real world experience spearheaded her cake and pie business and drove considerable sales.

Remember that older employees (and I am talking thirty and above) aren't always as moldable as younger inexperienced individuals and may "stick to their guns" on certain decisions rather than follow directions, particularly from younger employees and managers.

Life experience without a filter can also be problematic. I once walked in to one of our stores and overheard our mature aged manager talking about her recent hysterectomy to a somewhat frightened young man who had just come in for a frosty treat.

Boy Scouts and Girl Guides Association
By definition these are groups of youths that are willing to serve their fellow man. They are always prepared and generally mix very well with their peers. Remember though that Scouting is like a religion to a lot of the crew and when the annual Camporee or pack meeting comes around, they are going to want a leave of absence to go "walkabout."

"So called" Friends and Family
I called this pool the "so-called" friends and family because when things go wrong in the workplace, you will rapidly find that these relationships crumble pretty quickly.

Nothing ruins a long friendship than firing your neighbor's daughter because she was caught with her paws in the honey pot. Sure you can both smile and wave as if it never happened, but these types of events create small cracks in these relationships that human beings find hard to forget. Obviously these applicants become pre-qualified because you know them or their parents or family. Although there are really no conditions to the family or friendship relationship, you must draw a line in the sand when someone from these groups is now working for you.

I have had relatively good success with these applicants as long as there is a hard and fast line drawn at the threshold of the workplace. Over this line, the friend/friend relationship stops and the employer/employee relationship starts. All parties need to understand this stipulation and agree to the terms and conditions that apply to every other employee in the business. Your own family members need to understand this also.

Direct Family Members
I have had three of my five children work for me in various ways, shapes and forms, and to tell you the truth, it has been a valuable bonding and teaching experience. The opportunity to work and talk side by side with your children should be a memory that you will look back on with fondness.

One of the issues here is your ability to remain impartial. In most cases I treat my children like any other employee in my business, but in the same vein, there are perks for having your dad as your boss. Other employees need to understand this concept, but many rarely do.

The biggest issue I have found in having my children working in my business is the way the *other* employees treat your children. I have had several "chats" with the crew on how my children are to be treated in the workplace. I have no tolerance for the whole "boss' daughter" routine from other employees.

Oh and By the Way...

Mom or Dad asking for employment applications or whether their son or daughter could get a job in our business is a deal breaker. Hey, I know the very strong urge to get your kids motivated, up and out of the house. We have five beautiful children—four girls and one boy. We have tried to instill in our children the motivation to work hard and to appreciate the benefits of a good day's work for a good day's pay.

However, when the day comes that *I* am out asking businesses for applications for my kids, I am overlooking a major teaching moment in my child's employment experience. The feeling of accomplishment when a teen or young adult acquires their first job on their own motivation and effort is hard to put a value on.

So Mom or Dad, don't ask me for an application for your son or daughter to work in my business. You are cheating me out of a young person who really wants to work and excel in their upcoming employment experience.

A Sign of the Times

Posting a sign outside of your business, in the drive through or in the window can be a double-edged sword. On the positive side, you are casting in a pool of fish that already loves or patronizes your business. A small sign in the drive through is capturing the attention of people who are willing to pay for your product and service, and make no mistake, the public votes with their dollars. It would appear that you already have a loyal pool to fish from.

The downside of having a sign posted in your window is that it may give an impression that you are finding it hard to get employees at your business. This may actually be the truth but not the kind of information you want your regular customers to see. Obviously it depends on the size and text of the sign.

A sign painted in four-foot-high fluorescent lettering stating "NIGHT MANAGERS NEEDED — GOOD WAGES" can be a little off-putting to the general customer service experience. Also, a sign visible from the road may bring in every Tom, Dick and Harry and you don't want that either. (For more information on Tom, Dick and harry see chapter 5.)

In our St Louis location, we had a monument sign at the front of our building near the sidewalk. This sign was backlit and easily visible to the fifty thousand cars that passed each and every day. It was also right smack at the bus stop. One of our managers suggested that we use our monument sign to advertise position vacancies, but when I showed her the raggedy band of characters that stumbled off that bus every afternoon, she changed her tune.

Don't Go Chasing Waterfalls
Wiser words have never been sung. The ladies from TLC had it together when they gave the counsel to "just stick to the rivers and the lakes that you are used to."

As mentioned at the beginning of the chapter, you should already have a core of solid employees who can serve as guides to where the other big fish are. In the fifteen years I have worked in the retail environment, I have had a considerably higher strike rate of obtaining new hires from recommendations received from my current employees. However there needs to be some accountability in place.

As mentioned in my horror story, I have always held my employees somewhat accountable when recommending a family member or friend. Sure, it would be great to get one of my friends a job where I work, but in the back of my mind, I am always weary that if things go terribly wrong and the new hire blasts the door off the safe one night, I may be partially responsible.

This principle needs to be impressed on the "recommender's" mind. I have always told my crew that their reputation is also on the line with their recommendation. There is an upside to recommending a hardworking employee. Not only do you have the satisfaction that you got your friend a job, I generally give a signing bonus to the "recommender," which may be a movie ticket or a meal coupon somewhere. This is money well spent considering that the prospect is already qualified and you've saved yourself some valuable time.

Love Is in the Air
So this brings up the question of boyfriends, girlfriends and romantic liaisons in the workplace. Let's say you have a great employee who either wants to bring a boyfriend or girlfriend aboard or perhaps a situation where a romance develops between two employees. This is a little different than a brother, sister or friend recommendation and can have varying results in my experience.

However, these kind of relationships impact negatively in the workplace.

Either you have a scenario where the two can't work together on a shift because there is too much eyelash batting or muscle flexing getting in the way of work duties. Everyone else on these shifts gets pretty tired of picking up the slack. This also creates extra work for you in trying to schedule them on different shifts constantly.

Then there is the breakup blues and the complications that come as a result of relationships going pear shaped. Soon you have employees wearing t-shirts equivalent to "Team Brad" and "Team Jennifer," which distract from getting things done. When "young love" spawns from working together, I have usually found the time to sit down with the pair and re-explain the focus of work time during their shifts. Having these elements in your policy and procedure manuals can also save you a lot of time and effort.

Four Seas Ice Cream

Four Seas Ice Cream in Centerville, Massachusetts has been serving ice cream since 1934 and has refined the employee search process so well that out of the local high school graduating class of five hundred, Four Seas has employed the number 1, 2, 3, 4, 6, 7 and 8th placed students. In fact, most of their new employees are honor roll students who are hand-selected by the ownership. Even the fact that you are selected for an interview is a point worth mentioning on your resume.

Four Seas is a third-generation business currently owned and operated by Doug and Peggy Warren. Doug and his dad, Dick "Chief" Warren were both teachers and only recruit the best of the best. Local "advanced" teaching staff make recommendations as to who in their classes would make great employees based on work ethic, intelligence, personality and motivation. In fact for the most part, you need to be an honor roll student to work at Four Seas.

You might also sneak in if you have family working there. One family has two daughters working at Four Seas currently. They also had an older sister work there as well as their mother and father; that's where they met. Oh and did I mention an aunt, uncle and both grandparents also worked at Four Seas. Apart from Doug, there are two other third-generation workers in the business. Amazing!

Another local mom who worked at Four Seas has since sent five of her sons off to scoop ice cream as well. Many local married couples owe their introductions to this ice cream shop. Dick Warren even met his wife while they were working together.

What then creates such a legacy of successful employees and work ethic? One element is the selection principles we have discussed in this chapter being practically applied.

The other is how the owners at Four Seas treat their employees. More on that later.

Chapter 5   The Application

Before we jump into the actual application, I have a quick question for those of you who have your businesses up and running. How easy is it to get an application to work at your business? Can anyone simply walk off the street and ask for an application? Do you have a stack of crisp, freshly printed application forms ready to give out willy-nilly to anyone who asks?

If so, you may be doing yourself a great disservice. You see the easier it is for any Tom, Dick or Harry to get an application to work in your business, the more work you are going to have to do in filtering out those who you do not want working for you.

Let's say for argument sake you received one hundred applications in one month. Statistics show us that at least 60% of these applications will be shelved as not worth pursuing. The forty that are left you may interview for. Out of the forty interviews that you conduct, you may have twenty employees you feel will work well in your business.

Out of the twenty employees you have offered work to, five will probably not be the kind of people you thought they were and you will let them go.

Five may decide that this is not the kind of business they want to work in. Or they may get a better offer or circumstances may change and they will leave within a couple of months. This leaves ten good employees that you can add to your overall crew. Doesn't this seem like a lot of work? One hundred applications are whittled down over your valuable time and effort to ten quality employees.

Make 'em Work For It

One of the reasons this may be is because your application form or the ability to submit one is too easy. You often see a situation where someone desperate for work, and I mean any kind of work, will simply walk up and down the street, asking for applications in every business they walk into.

Some will even fill out the application while they're in your store and hand it back before smiling and walking onto the next business. Although this person's work seeking ethic should be applauded, may I suggest that this is not the employee you want. You want your employee to be motivated to work in your particular business. You want your potential applicants to seek you out among the myriad of other employment opportunities. This guy is just throwing enough mud up against the wall and seeing what sticks.

You want an employee who will be more motivated to work harder for you because she has an emotional investment in her employment. She sought *you* out. So how do you make people work harder to get a job with you? Well for a start you don't let your application be handed out willy-nilly like most other businesses.

The harder it is for applicants to submit an application, the more refined your employee potential pool will be. In most of our businesses we have had our application online, and just because the actual application is online does not mean it is able to be submitted online. If a potential employee lobs up at our counter and asks for an application for employment, this is the process he or she goes through.

Sorry, We Don't Have Applications Here.

Our potential applicants are informed that our application is on our website, and it will need to be printed, filled out and returned.

At this point we have discouraged all of those who either do not have a computer or could not be fazed to go back home, look up the site, print out the form, fill out the form and then return it to the store. I know that by the time someone has dropped off an application to the store, they have gone out of their way to do so. Believe it or not this probably weeds out about 30% of those who aren't really looking for a job in our store. They are just looking for a job for free ice cream.

Now let's talk about that application.

Legal Mumbo Jumbo

The first thing you will need to do is to ensure that your application is not discriminatory. I know that sounds crazy but some questions you ask on your application may be construed incorrectly and hence be illegal.

In some states you can't even ask whether the applicant has a driver's license. Believe it or not, this can be construed to mean that you will only employ people who have licenses and discriminate against those who don't or are not old enough to. You can however, ask how they are going to get to work.

All of these semantics can be very confusing for a business owner who just wants to put out an application form. Again, it would be good to run an example of your form past your attorney or the state Labor Department to make sure your form is compliant.

Most applications from here are pretty standard.

- Name
- Address
- Contact details
- SSN
- Previous Employment
- Availability

The "Not so Formal" Questions

Once the legal and common sense questions are on your application you may want to spice it up a little bit to reflect the kind of business or employer they will be working with.

We have questions like:

- What is your favorite song?
- Are you a dog or cat person?
- Your favorite flavor of ice cream?
- If you could have a super power, what would it be?
- What is your favorite Muppet? (Don't tell me you don't know who the Muppets are?)

Most applicants get a kick out of these questions and enjoy answering them. You will also see a new side of these applicants open up that you would not see in a general and boring job application. We have had super powers wished for like the standard "being able to fly" and "X-Ray vision" all the way up to "creating world peace" and "being able to shoot laser beams out of their eyes."

Getting an idea of their creativity and a look into how they might treat your customers and other employees are all rolled up in the answers to these fun questions.

The $64 Question

I also have a question on my application that probably tells me more about how motivated the applicant is than any other question. Accompanied with our application is a second document that asks the applicant to write a short essay or couple of paragraphs to answer this question.

Why do you want to work in our business?

I adopted this approach after seeing my good friend Steve Repucci from Mad Maggie's Ice Cream use it with great success. (Props to Steve.) Before we ask the applicant to write a couple of paragraphs, we explain what it is actually like to work in an ice cream store:

"Working in an ice cream shop looks like fun from the outside, but it's a lot of hard work. The customers can be demanding and there can be a lot of pressure. It is also mainly evening and weekend shifts so you have to work when other kids are out having fun. You also have to be willing to pick up trash, clean utensils, bathrooms, floors, etc. Do you think you can handle it?

Use the rest of this page to tell us why you think you will like it. You don't have to write a long essay — just a few sentences to tell us why you feel you'll enjoy being part of our team. We base a lot of our decision on how you answer this question."

As we explain, I go more from what is written on this document than I do from the actual application. A couple of forced sentences usually don't cut it here. If this young man or woman can't explain with some form of passion why they want to work in my shop, they certainly will not be able to treat my customers with the level of passion that I want them to have.

The Arts and Craft Show
There are many and varied ways to spice up the whole application process and get a real intrinsic view of how your potential hires think and solve problems.

I was recently in a business where I noticed shelves and shelves of what looked like an art and craft show. The sign posted above these creations read *"These are some Groovy Applications."* The application process at this shop is far different and creative than any other I have come across.

Applications made from paper bags

When an applicant asks for details about a job, they are first given a white paper bag and are told to create something with it. It doesn't necessarily have to be then and there. They can take it home and work on it. This idea is pure genius.

This employer wants a crew that is talented, creative and willing to have a go at anything. Some of the results of these paper bag creations are worthy of any art museum or display. Displaying them also shows customers the passion the employees have for the shop in which they work.

Sure you still need to know names, address and other details, however this first step will sift out the dude that simply wants free ice cream and a regular paycheck. Bringing a simple origami party hat or swan won't cut it at this business.

You will find an example of our application at www.hopelesstohero.com. Use it as a guide to fine-tune your own process and always check with the relevant Labor Department to ensure it complies with your local legislation.

Sifting through the Masses

So after the applications start rolling in, what do you do now?

How do you filter through the hundreds of applicants that want to work in your store? The last thing you want to do is interview every one of these applicants. The principle of adding a filter to these applications will help you sift out those who may not be suitable right from the word go. Remember the percentages we have touched on earlier. You will need to receive a lot of applications to eventually whittle them down to who you are going to interview and then to whittle down as to who you will actually hire, then whittle down to see if they actually are a good fit for your business.

So what kind of filters do you use to separate out the wheat from the chaff? When you are opening up a new retail location, it is not unusual to be inundated with applications to work at your store. At our pilot location in Brisbane, Australia, we had about 130 applications to rummage through.

Our second location was a kiosk in one of the largest shopping malls in our city—a real hangout for the youth of that area. When we started building this location, we received over three hundred applications. That's a lot of time and effort to weed out about twenty or thirty applicants to interview.

Whether you are sifting through three hundred applications or just thirteen, here are a couple of tips that have saved me a lot of time over the years.

The Performers

I want someone who can perform well—someone who isn't shy or afraid to stand up in front of relative strangers and present a cheery countenance and good attitude to the paying public. So as I sift through the pile, I put aside those applicants who play a musical instrument, are involved in local theatre or an acting club at school and those who may be in the debating or speech programs at their educational institutions. These folks have already honed the craft of "performing" in front of a crowd and usually have developed a good sense of self-confidence and awareness.

School Locations

Most retail locations will end up hiring teens between sixteen and twenty as the core base of their employees. Where possible you need to spread these applicants over multiple high schools.

As previously mentioned, the problem with getting all of your employees from one school is that whenever there is a big event like homecoming or prom, you may find yourself working your own business alone that day or two. Spreading employees between different school locations gives you better coverage overall.

Sports

You may think that someone who is involved heavily in sporting activities would also fall in this category. Surely this type of applicant is a team player who can work together with those around them to achieve a common goal. This may be the case, however you may find that as this kind of applicant dedicates more time and effort to their sporting pursuits, they may request more and more time off.

One of our better employees ascended the ranks of field hockey in our state. She was a great employee (when she was available) however multiple nights a week of practice and traveling to local regional and state hockey events left us a little short with her availability. We tried to work around her schedule when we could, but she eventually resigned so she could concentrate on her passion.

Field of Study

Identifying the passions, interests and fields of study that a potential employee is focusing on can also add a dual value to their employment. As previously stated, students or individuals who have a passion for marketing, social media, public relations, or accounting can assist you in the day-to-day operations and promotions of your business. These are all functions that you or someone you delegate will have to perform. Why not utilize slow times to have employees with a set of skills or passion assist in the fulfillment of these tasks.

Having the application and the filters to fine tune the list for your interviewing process will certainly help you. Oh and by the way, before the applications start rolling in, you should also be very aware of the types of people who will be applying for your vacancies.

Chapter 6   Types of Employees

Just so you understand, kids these days are more driven, responsible, educated, tech savvy, emotional, introverted and crazy than any other generation. I have tried to wrap my head around the types of people I have had working for me over the years. It hasn't been easy but I think I have it figured out.

You staff members will more than likely fall into the following categories:

- o   Sleepers
- o   Creepers
- o   Peepers
- o   Weepers
- o   Leapers
- o   Jeepers Creepers and
- o   Keepers

Sleepers

The sleeper is the staff member who looks for every opportunity to sit and rest. The motto "Time to lean is time to clean" is far from his thought process. In fact, his time to lean is practically his whole shift. This is the guy who puts great effort in memorizing the owner's personal vehicle—make, model and license plate number. He also knows the make and type of the owner's wife's car, his mother's car and several of the owner's closest friends.

I was doing some consulting in a national franchise store when the word "HUMMER!" was yelled at the top of one sleeper's voice. Everyone jumped into action and all of a sudden, the workplace became a hive of activity. I later learned the owner of this business drove a Hummer and that was the signal that called all and sundry to action when he drove into the parking lot.

The sleeper has perfected the "Cockroach Scramble." Ever walked into a darkened room and turned on the lights to find cockroaches scampering to the nearest dark hiding place. Well this employee will sit and chat to anyone within the range of his voice until the owner or manager's car appears. Then it is "*action all stations*" and he is up and about before you can say Jack Robinson.

The very dangerous principle of the sleeper is that he is infectious. A good conversation usually needs at least two people to participate, and once the sleeper initiates what he does best, others usually succumb and join the sleeper's lackadaisical state. You've got to get rid of this guy or reform him quickly. He is the bad apple that will spoil the bunch.

Creepers

The creeper is genuinely a good employee. He is relatively competent and will do as you direct. He is capable of working unsupervised, is well presented and punctual. His only downfall is he is working at one tenth of the capacity of everyone else. He will eventually get the job done, but by the time completion has come around, so has Christmas. Now the creeper is not a lost cause, so don't give up. Many of his work ethics and characteristics are valuable; he just needs a little motivation to move the job along.

The game of test cricket is a classic example of creeping. These games can last up to five days and it is not unusual to hear the spectators start "*The Slow Hand Clap*." This clap usually starts off nice and slow, however over a period of about thirty seconds builds up in sound and pace until it resembles a string of firecrackers igniting. This is what the creeper needs. Start the "*Slow Hand Clap*" in his presence and gradually build up speed until, he too, is moving at a feverish pace.

Peepers

These employees are so entitled because you rarely hear a peep out of them. They have all of the desirable traits of the creeper and can even move in the same time zone as the rest of the world, but through shyness or low self-confidence, find it hard to raise more than a mumble to your customers.

You can usually pick the peepers out in the interview process. The peepers tend to not make eye contact and talk very quietly and deliberately. They rarely give themselves praise and often look for opportunities to do inventory or wash putrefied trashcans out rather than greet a customer. But hey...someone has to do inventory and wash putrefied trashcans, so don't discount them.

If you have a few peepers on board the good ship, try and praise them whenever you can. "Wow, this trash can is so clean, I could eat off it" They may never be your public relations specialists, but they will work hard for you in a less confronting field.

Weepers

It's a good thing to be in touch with your emotions, that's why we were blessed with them. And we all have bad days mixed in with the good, but the workplace is not the place to let the emotional meltdown occur. Although these are unavoidable from time to time, a repeat weeper can really be a thorn in your side. Overly emotional employees can be a drain on you, your other staff members and even your customers. I came in to our ice cream store one afternoon to overhear one staff member discussing the rigors of her recent boyfriend breakup with a customer. Hey, I don't mean to sound unsympathetic, but find a qualified professional outside of work hours to talk to!

Now you may bring some of this weeping onto yourself. I try not to be discriminatory in my employment when it comes to males vs. females, but as it turns out, in a store of about twenty employees, most times about nineteen of them were girls and one was a boy. He was just there to lift heavy stuff. Girls generally are more mature, punctual and reliable. They iron their clothes, scrub under their nails and care about the way they look before leaving the house. The challenge you have will be the high amounts of estrogen in the workplace with all of these girls.

As a father of five children, four of them daughters, believe me—I speak from experience.

Leapers
The leaper is almost the opposite of the peeper. He exudes self-confidence and is always looking for the next hurdle to soar over. This is an admirable quality nonetheless, but sometimes he is really not that keen to perform the mundane duties he is assigned to do. He is always looking to create the next menu item or coming up with the next great idea to move your business to the next level rather than mop the floor or take out the trash. And not that you want to stem his creative genius either, but there needs to be moderation in all things.

The unleashed leaper can very easily turn into a jeepers creeper (*See Jeepers Creepers*). So take the time to praise his enthusiasm and vision, but all the while teach him that there are some tasks, however unpleasant or routine, that need to be done. And sometimes, he's just the guy to do it.

Now the team up of a leaper and a peeper on the same shift can sometimes work very effectively, but the leaper does need to be taught that there comes a time in every man's life when you just got to clean the toilet yourself.

Jeepers Creepers

This category is set aside for the above-mentioned employees who let their specific tendencies get out of control. It is also for the freaks, geeks and outright insane. Most of the jeepers creepers never get past the interview stage.

Sometimes, you may come across the "sleeper jeepers creeper." Now the word "sleeper" is not used here as denoted in our first category. This is the jeepers creeper in embryo. This is the respectable employee who decides on a whim to go and get a green Mohawk or thirty-seven facial piercings during a night out with the boys. This is why your staff handbook is never set in concrete. Now you never thought to add a "Radical Haircut Policy" at the time of printing, but maybe that might not be such a bad idea!

Always keep in mind that any employee in another category has the potential to morph into a jeepers creeper so keep a close eye on them.

Keepers

Well, as the term denotes, these are the staff members who you could trust with your first-born. They are not experts in all fields, but they have a good level of competency in most fields. They have it together in punctuality, dress, attitude, honesty, work ethic and reliability.

Keepers are the staff members who allow you to take a step back from your business and spend some quality time with the bookwork, developing a marketing plan, or spending some much needed time with the family (and not in that particular order). Keepers tend to not be pigeon-holed to a certain age, marital status or job description. You can find, develop or mold a "keeper" from any of the lumps of clay working in your business. Now the secret of developing a staff load of keepers is found in the environment you create within the workforce.

Most of your help has a little "keeper" inside them—the little seed that wants to break through the soil of containment and blossom into a beautiful flower. It is up to you to nourish that little seed.

There's a Fine Line between Pleasure and Pain.

Creating a sales team that has outgoing and bubbly personalities can also have its drawbacks. Often times, the staff member who possesses these characteristics can walk the fine line between entertaining and downright annoying.

I recall waiting on a small airplane to take off from Escanaba, Michigan. It was a twin prop model with a single row of about ten seats on either side of the cabin. Sitting right in front of me was a gentleman in his early thirties, sporting an extremely high Mohawk hairdo. I immediately thought that anyone that age with such an extreme head of hair must have a few loose roof tiles.

In any case, the plane started filling up slowly with other passengers until about four or five other pilots, in full uniform boarded the plane and moved to the rear of the cabin. The pilot and co-pilot still had the cockpit door open while completing some preflight checks, when this guy called out, "Gee, you guys really look after your passengers. Look at all of these back up pilots!"

Well, this comment drew a substantial amount of laughter from both the pilots and the other passengers. I even had a chuckle myself. Obviously this guy felt he was on a roll and commenced calling out the most annoying, non-humorous comments over the following ten minutes.

What sort of meal are we getting on this flight?
Are we going to hit Mach 2 today?
Do you need me to flap my wings to help us along?

Eventually the pilots closed the cockpit door without comment, and the rest of us in the captive audience looked longingly out of the windows. If one of your staff members is this guy in embryo, it's time to take him aside and straighten him out. Remember, it's great to be friendly with your staff, but you're not in this business to make friends. You're here to create an exciting and entertaining destination for your customers.

Chapter 7   The Audition

Yes that's right—the audition. That's what it needs to be. When you are in the process of hiring new people, you want them to perform, to "earn" the privilege of working in your establishment.

I spoke to a young woman who applied for a job as an assistant bookkeeper in a large casino. After her potential employer reviewed her written application, she was given the opportunity to come to the casino for an interview. When she arrived early for this interview, she noticed numerous other applicants, both men and women waiting in the large auditorium.

There were others waiting to apply for the position she was there for, and quite a few more waiting for interviews for two other positions. Once all of the applicants had arrived and registered, a panel of three interviewers sat in the front and divided the large group into two smaller groups. Then came the shocking announcement:

"The group on my left will now hop on the stage and do the chicken dance. The group on my right will be doing the Hokey Pokey shortly afterwards."

A stunned silence came over the room as the few chuckles petered out. After what seemed to be an eternity, a solemn mood settled when all in attendance realized this wasn't a joke. Some got up and walked out, mumbling under their breaths words to the effect of "What the hell does dancing have to do with bookkeeping?"

Actually, dancing has everything to do with the situation. No, the chicken dance won't enhance your capability to complete a profit and loss sheet more effectively, but it does tell you employer a bit about your character.

It also tells you a lot about the environment you will be working in. Sure accounting isn't the most dynamic career choice, but obviously this employer values fun, communication and participation in their workspace. The more people who got up and walked out, the better it was for the panel of interviewers. It was like contestants voting themselves off the island.

Long story short, after a couple of rounds of party dancing and crazy folk tunes, my friend got the job. The moral of this story is that you shouldn't settle for less than your standard and your applicant should feel it a privilege to vie for a position in your business. A quick word of advice—please reread chapter 3 to ensure that asking potential employees to dance before you is not against the law.

Try explaining that one to your spouse? "Oh Honey, it's not such a big deal—I just asked a bunch of teenagers to dance for me?"

Some Pre-Interview Tips

It is always good to schedule the interview at your shop or business. This is important for a number of reasons, but the most important of all, is that you are the King of the Jungle here. It is essential for your potential hire to see you roaming and ruling in your natural environment. It also gives them an opportunity to see and get the feel for the surroundings.

I have often heard of the principle of conducting group interviews. This is where you would invite four or five hopefuls and pose questions to the group rather than the individual. This process allows you to see who domineers the conversation, or perhaps identify the shy and quiet ones. I will say that I have never conducted these types of interviews, as I prefer the one on one process.

Never Imply Someone Has the Job before the Interview

Never give someone the impression that you are going to give them the job before the Interview. No matter who they are—friends, family, friends of family, family of friends—it doesn't matter. Every person who comes in for an interview needs to be of the mindset that there are others vying for that position and may be better qualified than they are.

Crazy Golf balls

When bunched all together on one interview day, your prospective employees can be kind of like a bag of golf balls. They may look similar on the outside but somewhere in the bunch, there may be a couple of those trick golf balls.

You know—the ones that aren't always balanced on the inside and always trail off in another direction. Or the ones that explode with the slightest contact. They are in there all right, and it's your job to sift them out through the interview process so you aren't left looking like a goose on the opening day of the tournament—if you know what I mean.

So your first task is coming up with a group of questions that will achieve the following objectives:

1. Make the interviewee feel as comfortable as they can
2. Help you establish the potential worker's strengths and weaknesses
3. Extract all of the information you need to make an informed decision

Might I suggest that if you fail in your first objective—you will fail in all three? A job interview is probably one of the most stressful fifteen to twenty minutes of anyone's life, closely followed by a driving test. And I should know. I had three of them! (Driving tests, not job interviews.) You need to understand that the more comfortable the interviewee is, the better the interview will go.

I can recall, sitting outside a convening panel room for a promotion within the police force I once belonged to. I knew that I was going to be asked a list of personal, procedural and law questions, which mind you, I did study for, but was extremely nervous about. Some of these statutes and procedure books are as thick as the Bible and memorizing all of what needs to be known can be a challenge.

To my complete surprise, the panel convener came out about ten minutes before the interview was to commence and gave me the list of questions that were going to be asked. He explained to me as he handed me the document that it would do no good for the panel and no good for me if I didn't feel comfortable enough to give a true indication of my knowledge and skills and not waste my time trying to memorize statutes and procedures that would not be asked about in the interview.

The same goes for your interviewee. Do all you can to help them feel comfortable and they will give you a clearer picture as to what they will be able to do for you as an employee.

Always Do the Interview Yourself
One of the challenges of being a business owner is the principle that the buck stops with you. Employing your crew is one of them. You will find that if you delegate this authority to the general manager or

anybody else for that matter, you may find yourself in a bind of having crewmembers who just don't work for you. This will only drive a wedge between the general manager, the employee and yourself. You may delegate bookwork, inventory or even some community events, but interviewing your future employees is something you should be doing personally.

Again, I can't stress this enough. These potential employees will stand at a register or somewhere in your business and represent you. You should have a say in who represents you, no? If a production company was pitching a movie about your life, I think you would have a short list as to what Hollywood movie stars you would like to play you. You should have the same say as to who "plays" you in your business.

Prep Time

There will be some preparation you will need to do in order to be ready for these interviews. One step you will need to strike off the list is calling the references that your applicant provides. I know, I know. No one is going to give you their parole officer as a reference. Or the guy they shanked on the train last week.

Here's the thing, though. Calling the reference sets a pattern and expectation for future employment. Say for example, Shelly gives you the number of her sweet granny that she takes to the market every Saturday as a reference. Of course Granny is going to give a glowing report of little Shelly and how reliable she is. You expect that. However, what most employers don't count on is that straight after you hang up the phone with Granny, what is Granny going to do? She is going to call Shelly and tell her the nice man from the ice cream shop called.

This sends an indirect message to your potential hire that you are an employer who follows up on information given to you. Granted, in this litigious society we now live in, it is becoming rare to find an ex-employer or associate who is willing to give you any information on account of divulging information that could get him or her in hot water. If you are speaking to an old employer of your prospect, generally the main question to ask is:

"Would you hire this person again if you had the chance?" The answer, though not rich in detail, should tell you a lot.

Create a Checklist
Create a question sheet to prompt you to ask the right questions. You will also need to make sure the questions you ask in the interview are legal and not discriminatory. Again, a quick call to the state or area Labor Relations Office will help you access those local laws.

You may also rely on a solicitor or legal representative to pass these questions off. As previously mentioned, never take for granted hiring regulations or receive advice from other business owners in this regard. Labor Department fines can be some of the biggest you will encounter and have been the demise of many a business not in compliance with the law.

After going through the details on the application, I generally use questions like the following:

- *What are your hobbies/interests?*
  This gets the applicant talking about their own likes and dislikes and generally breaks the ice for the rest of the questions

- *What are your plans for school/college/university?*

  Again, another slow ball although this will be a good indication so far as availability and motivation to work in your business.

- *Do you have any other work experience?*

  I am generally not too fussed on previous work experience. It is not a deal breaker for me that an applicant has not had formal experience in the work place. For those who have, this is obviously a look into their experience and capabilities.

- *Have you ever worked in the food industry?*

  The foodservice and restaurant industry provides some of the toughest working environments available. Applicants who have experience in these environments have typically been trained to some degree and worked in stressful and challenging environments.

- *Do you like cleaning?*

  This is a good one. I don't recall an applicant in the hundreds I have interviewed that ever said they don't like cleaning. I usually back their response up with, *"If your mom was here would she agree with you?" This* question may be tongue in cheek, but it does send a message that part of their responsibilities could be cleaning—a lot of cleaning.

- *When are you available for work?*
- *How many hours would you like per week?*

  These two questions sound the same but have very different meanings. You can have an applicant seated across from you who claims to have total availability. *"I'm not going to college this semester, so the world is my oyster."*

"How many hours do you want per week?"

"Well maybe four or five — let's not get crazy here!"

- *Do you have any concerns about working here?*
  This is my favorite question of all. This is you your coverall question in case there are any little questions or concerns hanging out there.

I conducted a training session in Washington State many years ago where a crew of fresh faced, newly hired employees were learning the ropes of a particular style of ice cream. As we were giving out samples, one young man protested and said, *"I can't eat ice cream—I'm a vegan!"*

"What's a vegan?" the owner asked me.

I shrugged my shoulders and said, *"Beats me."*

That was my first foray into the vegan way of life. The owner said—

"I don't think you can work here if you can't eat the ice cream."

"Well...I'm kind of a vegan!"

"What does that mean?"

"Well, I have this really hot girlfriend, and she is vegan, so I said I was too. I guess I will eat it if you are going to throw it out!"

No doubt one of the weirder exchanges I have heard during training sessions. Now this concern perhaps, should have been brought up in the interview. With a question about any outstanding comments or concerns, that is a good area to wrap things up.

Other Considerations

Remember that open-ended questions always solicit a better response. Any questions that can be answered with a yes or a no tend to stifle the conversation and fail to draw out vital information about the applicant.

You may also consider throwing in the follow suggested questions to help in the selection process:

- *Tell me a bit about yourself.*
- *What are you most proud of?*
- *What are your strengths or weaknesses?*
- *Where do you see yourself in a couple of years?*
- *What did you like least about your last job?*
- *How do you take constructive criticism?*
- *Have you ever worked with someone you didn't like? How did you handle that?*
- *Do you have any questions for me?*
- *What type of music to you like?*
- *If you could have a super power what would it be?*
- *Are you a dog or cat person?*
- *What is your favorite song right now?*
- *If you could play a musical instrument what would it be?*

These last questions give the applicant a sense of what it would be like working in this environment. We have used this information on our store website when describing the kind of person who works for us.

The Job Entails...

It is also a good idea to have a printed job description on hand to go through with the applicant. I don't pull these out for everyone. If the interview isn't going well from my perspective and I have made my mind up that this isn't the person for me, it is a waste of time to talk about what duties the job entails. However, if an applicant looks promising I will share this document with them to give them an idea of what they can expect working in our establishment.

You may find having a list of core duties on hand will also be helpful. Points such as:

- *Customer Service*
- *Cash handling*
- *Cleaning*
- *Food preparation*
- *Product making*
- *Cleaning*
- *Marketing/Promotion duties*
- *Cleaning and*
- *Cleaning*

Give Yourself a Couple of Minutes between Interviews

Like I stated previously, if you have more than two applicants you are interviewing in a certain time period, give yourself some time to make some notes about the applicant. I generally rate them in three areas:

1. Personality
2. Appearance
3. Confidence

Make some notes on the application or question sheet for later review. Have you ever walked out of a movie and thought you might go any see another straight away. After doing so, try and remember anything about the first movie. Thus it is with employee interviews.

Call Backs

I never tell someone they have the job at the interview. One of the main reasons for this is that I would never tell anyone that they didn't have the job at the interview. Imagine the demoralization at the end of an interview that you think is going pretty well to be told *"Well thanks for coming in, but you didn't get the job."*

Even when I only have one person I am interviewing, I generally contemplate the conversation and my thoughts before advising the applicant of the result.

And don't cop out by not calling the one you did not select. A very gentle and dignified *"I'm sorry but we have filled all our positions for this period. We will keep you application of file should be need to contact you"* will save you multiple calls from the individual (or his/her parents) or an inbox full of emails from desperate hanger-on-ers.

Following these simple steps will have you leaps and bounds ahead of the competition in regards to having a crew that represents yourself and your product to the highest standards. As mentioned in my Horror Story (chapter 2) rushing through this process or not taking the time to ensure all of these elements are in play can not only save you time, but effort and money as well.

Chapter 8   The Mission Statement

I know, even the term "Mission Statement" conjures up buzz words of the late 1980s and early 1990s like "synergy" and "paradigm," however I can tell you from personal experience that a well-crafted mission statement can not only benefit you and your employees, but ultimately will benefit your customers as well.

Your statement should cover in basic and plain terms your reason for being in business and the experience your employees and your customers will experience by being involved.

Your Mission, Should You Choose to Accept It

Recently we had a large and spacious gym open up close to our home. It is a monster. When the building was first under construction, I thought it was going to be a shopping mall due to its sheer enormity.

It has got everything in there—hairdresser, rock-climbing walls, indoor and outdoor pools with slides and water parks, the whole shebang. The café is also well tricked out with an expansive menu of kids' meals and nutritious servings for weight watching adults. One item that always impressed me when I first went in there was the plaque on the wall by the water dispensers. It reads:

"LifeCafe promises a menu that is good for you and delicious with service that is friendly and fast."

In one simple statement, the management has captured their mission, both for their customers and their staff members. As a customer, I get a "warm and fuzzy" because I see that this establishment is striving for excellence in product and service. Hopefully for the staff members working there, it is a constant reminder of the standards that their employer requires of them.

A simple mission statement can do that for *your* business also. You don't need to be a large franchise chain, a fancy gym or any multi-unit operation to have a statement of what you hope to achieve for your customers, your employees and yourself.

I know what you are thinking—this "airy fairy" "Nancy boy" stuff isn't for me. Well *not* having a Mission Statement may do more harm than good. In fact not having any established goals and priorities for your business is kind of like starting the car you just spent an exorbitant amount of money on, putting your foot on the accelerator and letting go of the steering wheel. Direction is a key principle for any business in any field. It is a necessity for you as the owner. Your managers need it to run your shop effectively and your employees crave it. In a recent convention in New Hampshire, I conducted a survey of the three principles small business owners felt were most important to the success of their business. The top three by an overwhelming margin were as follows:

1. Customer service
2. Shop cleanliness and atmosphere
3. Quality of the menu items

I would imagine these principles are also important to you. Some other principles that may be important to your business could be:

1. Community involvement
2. Value for money
3. Presentation of your menu items or services
4. Fund raising for local charities
5. Fun and entertainment
6. Clean bathrooms

Whenever we open a new location, we spend some dedicated time going over this thought process and formulating a mission statement that will not only keep our crew heading in the right direction, but will also serve as a marketing tool for our customers.

We had our mission statement printed, framed and mounted on the wall close to our registers where it would be most visible to our customers. It reads:

Our Mission

Mr. C's Ice Cream Emporium will provide its customers with a unique Ice Cream experience based on:

➤ Value, Quality and Presentation of Product,
➤ Excellence in Customer Service and a
➤ Clean Fun and Entertaining Atmosphere.

If your ice cream experience is any less than this, please let a member of our management know. We value your opinion and your business.

Again, our statement focused on three principles that we felt were very important to the success of our business. Our menu items, our customer service and our customer environment.

You may find that as your responsibilities and concepts grow, so might your missions and goals. Ben and Jerry's Ice Cream in the USA have expended their reach far beyond just making great ice cream. In fact their mission statement covers three separate and distinct areas of focus.

Their **social mission** is as follows:
"To operate the company in a way that actively recognizes the central role that business plays in society by initiating innovative ways to improve the quality of life locally, nationally and internationally."

Their **product mission** is a little different:
"To make, distribute and sell the finest quality, all natural ice cream and euphoric concoctions with a continued commitment to incorporating wholesome, natural ingredients and promoting business practices that respect the Earth and the Environment."

And finally their **economic mission**:
"To operate the company on a sustainable financial basis of profitable growth, increasing value for our stakeholders and expending opportunities for development and career growth for our employees."

Quite the mouthful, and certainly a little more complex then when two young lads started selling ice cream bars out of the trunk of their car.

Still, for the most part, you can start very simply, as we did. After putting it up on the wall, I was surprised at the response from those in our business. Many of our customers waiting for service would read our statement and comment how nice it was to see a business striving for a high standard.

Yes we have had some customers pull us up on some of the principles. The odd customer may mention to our manager that they felt they waited too long for their order to be made. Some of these complaints were bona fide and others were just frivolous. Regardless of their origin, these conversations were motivated by the concept of making our business the best ice cream shop in town. Here are our customers talking to us about our business. That's always a positive. When your customers engage in a quest to try and improve your business, they feel a kind of "emotional ownership" in the progress of the shop. Let me share with you two examples where our humble Mission Statement hanging on the wall resulted in dramatic changes in our business.

The Mr. C's Freeze.

Recently we had a customer recommend a menu item after looking at our Mission Statement. She noted our first point that focused on quality of product. She recalled that she had enjoyed a particular menu item at another business and recommended that we serve it. I don't know her name but she pulled up in a pink Cadillac so I know she had achieved considerable success in the Mary Kay organization.

"You guys should have an arctic blast."
"What is an arctic blast?" I asked.
"Well its ice cream blended in a cup with a slushee."

We went to work experimenting with the two ingredients while she waited and supervised the research and development project. After several failed attempts and playing with several ratios, we handed over the final prototype.

A smile came to her face. "That's it!" she exclaimed.

In fact, after she had paid for it, she immediately opened the lid and offered all of the employees a taste of her creation. It was pretty good. I told her if she could come up with the great name for the item, we would put it on the menu. She knitted her brow for about twenty seconds while the cogs were turning and finally blurted out, *"The Mr. C's Freeze!"*

Bingo! We have a winner! That was amazing. It's now on the menu and I am sure she has told more than a handful of her associates that her efforts have been rewarded with a dedicated space on our menu board. That's the ultimate emotional ownership—right there.

Sometimes the mission statement on the wall can highlight some of the deficiencies in your operations that need to be corrected.

The Back Room Bandits

In one location, we had a rear storeroom that was separated from the general employee work area by a doorway. This door was usually left open throughout the day to allow free access to the storeroom for restocking items and such.

On this one particular day, a young mom came in to treat her two young children with an ice cream. When they entered the store, the door buzzer went off to indicate to our employees that customers were "incoming." For whatever reason the two employees in the back storeroom did not hear the buzzer and the customer was left standing by herself at the register.

After calling out a couple of times, our crewmembers apologized for the delay, took her order and processed her payment. As the young family went outside to the outdoor dining area, my distracted duo returned to the back room. Upon realizing that she needed a couple more spoons, the customer returned to the counter and repeated the process of calling out for assistance. Unbelievable right?

Not getting any response, she spotted the spoons over the counter and in disgust, reached over past the register to get the spoons herself. As she reached, she noticed the Mission Statement hanging on the wall. The words *"Excellence in Customer Service"* jumped out at her.

Upon returning home, she went to our website and emailed me regarding the experience. I replied that I appreciated her conveying her thoughts, that I valued her business and sent her a couple of free cone coupons. The two employees didn't get the same kind of warm and fuzzy communication.

From that day onward, we changed our policy that the door to the storeroom was to remain closed during the opening hours of the business and employees must be either directed by a manager to be there or be on a designated break. I shudder to think that this customer would think that this level of service was the norm in our business or even worse, relate this tale to her friends and relatives.

When is the best to create, or refine your Mission Statement? Right now! It will be time well spent, not only for your employees, but for your customers' overall experience and your business in general.

Chapter 9   The Policy and Procedure Handbook

I will not delve too deeply into this important document in this work, as there can be a whole separate volume written in relation to the policy and procedure manuals (and probably will). That being said, I can not underscore the need for this living and breathing document to be a key component in your business. And not just for employee training, but in the day-to-day operations of your business.

If you do not have an up-to-date policy and procedure manual for your business, you have no clear direction or boundaries for your employees.

What He Said and What They Heard

I once stood by a new storeowner during his first staff training meeting, and I was shocked at the events that were unfolding before my eyes. Not only did he not have a handbook ready to go over, he was making up policy as he went along. What was worse is that his new employees knew it. As he rolled through the hastily developed policies, I watched each employee and wondered what they were really hearing as he went through point by point.

He said - *"Umm you guys can eat whatever you want, when you want because I know you are going to be sick of it soon and you won't want anymore."*

What they heard - *"You guys can eat whatever you want, when you want, and if you can't eat it, just give it to your friends."* Some may have heard, *"Our product doesn't really have much value so wasting it or giving it away isn't really a big deal."*

<u>What he should have said</u> – *"I am happy for you to make a sundae or other menu item that you would like at the end of your shift, however you need to take it out with you. If you would like to give it to a family member or friend, that's OK. After you have finished work, you can do whatever you would like with it. If you give it to someone during your shift, it may be perceived that you are giving product away for free; just one item per shift and no rain checks. If you don't want something after a particular day, it doesn't carry over to another day. Does anyone have any questions?"*

<u>He said</u> - *"I need you to show up to work on time."*

<u>They heard</u> – *"I need you to walk in the door on time with your apron over your shoulder, put your bag in the back, talk to a few co-workers and then be ready to serve some customers."*

<u>What he should have said</u> – *"If you are scheduled to start work at 10 a.m., I need you to be standing at the register, apron on and ready to serve customers at 10 a.m. For this to happen, you probably need to get in ten minutes early so you can look presentable and be ready.*

<u>He said</u> – *"Can you let me know when you are calling in sick."*

<u>They heard</u> – *"Can you let me know when you are calling in sick? As close to starting time is fine because I can always call someone else on a whim and have them replace you."*

<u>What he should have said</u> – *"I need to know as soon as possible if you are sick. I know some illnesses can come on quickly but the*

sooner I know, the sooner I can make some calls to have someone replace you."

You see, if you are pulling policies out of the air and wording them in such a way that comes across as ambiguous or obscure, you are destined for an uphill battle with your employees. Take the time to develop and type a document that will affect the efficiency and effectiveness of your workforce. Without this document you are floating in the vast ocean of business with no firm rudder to keep you going in the right direction.

That's not to say that if you do have an employee manual that you won't endure some of the storms or tempests that will challenge your resolve. It just means you have a plan in place before the winds start to howl.

What Your Handbook Should Say

Most employee handbooks or policy and procedure manuals are broken up into three sections:

- Legal or Local Authority Policy
- Employee benefits
- General Business Policy

Legal or Local Authority Policy

You will note that some policies are mandated by your local labor health or safety departments. These policies may include:

Discrimination/Harassment
Employee Uniforms and Presentation

Personal Hygiene

Hand Washing Techniques

Glove Policy

Handling of Money

Employee Schedule

Employee Discipline

Employee or Customer Injury

As mentioned in some of the earlier chapters of this book, particularly chapter 3, the majority of these policies will already be written out and mandated by state or federal law, so you should not have to reinvent the wheel. Your biggest challenge here is compliance. Ensure that you have legislation that is up to date and current so that you don't fall foul of the law.

You will find that most of these procedures are not available in written form but more so available on websites and whitepapers. This is to prevent issuing or circulating documents that have been superseded by new or current policies and statutes. Having these policies printed out in your policy and procedure manuals or on an employee noticeboard is a necessary evil. Regular checks on state department websites and bulletins are a must to ensure you are posting and following current guidelines.

Employee Benefits

There will also be policies that apply directly to employee benefits. These policies may overlap with some local authority recommendations but have direct application to your employees and their benefits for working in your business.

Some examples of these policies are:

Employee Meals and Breaks

Employee Discounts

Vacation

Sick Leave

Payroll

Employee Probation

There may be some crossover here with those policies that are mandated by law so the same principles apply as with the first category. Also remember that some employees are more vocal about breaches of these kinds of policies than others. Some crewmembers will call you late at night if there is even a hint that they were underpaid for the last pay period (you never usually hear back if there was an over payment).

Other more passive employees may not mention smaller infractions until the molehill has grown into a mountain and soon you have angry parents or even worse, the Workplace Relations department knocking on your door. Best policy here is to get it right the first time and maintain your communication with the crew regarding discrepancies in pay or conditions.

General Business Policy

The remainder of the policies will be your guidelines as to how you want your business to run and your employees to work within that framework. The balance may not be necessarily mandated by local guidelines or apply to the benefit program of your crew.

These are the items that you, as the business owner want to have in place to maximize employee performance and have your business run smoothly. Examples of these policies may include:

Time Clock and Attendance
Theft
Honesty and Accountability
Employee Suggestions/Reports
Cell Phones and Personal Belongings
Loitering Behind the Counter
Appropriate Language
Smoking and Chewing Tobacco
Shop Security
Confidentiality
Customer Complaints and Daily Log
Everything Else

As I have mentioned a couple of times, this must be a living, breathing document and be updated with every odd situation or occurrence that you didn't count on or would never have believed would happen at your business.

Never Underestimate the Power of Stupid

Many of you could (and probably have) told stories of employee stupidity and monumental lapses of judgment, hence the need to review and update your employee manual at least annually. Let me give you a sample of some acts of stupidity that I never would have thought to include in a first round draft of my employee manual.

I was working in one of our locations one particular morning, when a regular customer, a bank manager, came in for his daily smoothie. You could almost set your watch by this guy. He certainly was very hung up on our smoothies and I always took the time to chitchat with him while he was in the store. This one particular day while I was making his smoothie, he said in passing, and I quote, *"The guy from the bike shop made me a great smoothie yesterday."* That tweaked my interest and I asked him what he meant. I don't mean to Tarantino this story but this is how the whole thing went down.

The manager on the day before this event was Carrie. Carrie was a relatively good employee and obviously of such a character that we would give her a key to the store and let her run a shift by herself. I don't know what was going through Carrie's head at the time. Maybe it was the worry that comes from a late fee on a particular bill, but she was panicking that she hadn't made a particular bill payment that day. Enter the guy from the bike shop. He was also one of our regular smoothie customers and would often refer other customers to us for our delicious drinks. He is what I would call a great ambassador.

Carrie, seeing the opportunity to make a quick exit to pay her bill, asked the guy from the bike shop if he wouldn't mind tending the store. And in one fluid movement, she turned, grabbed her purse and ran out the door. The bike shop guy stood there—alone and dumbfounded. Before he had had a chance to compose himself and reflect on this peculiar situation, enter the bank manager.

"Where is the smoothie girl?" asks the bank manager.
"I guess she went out to pay a bill."
The bank manager looks at his watch and exclaims, "That's a shame I really wanted a smoothie today."

The guy from the bike shop perks up and proudly proclaims, "*I can make you a smoothie.*" The bike shop guy then proceeds to walk around the counter, scoop some ice cream, put it in a jug with fruit and base and by all accounts blended up a pretty good smoothie.

At this point, he has more value to me as an employee than Carrie does. Now I mention the story because despite your best efforts in policy and procedures, there will still be times when you will scratch your head and think, "Want on earth is going through these people's minds?" It would have never entered my mind to put into the employee manual "Please don't leave the store while there are customers in the store and no other employees are working."

But we had to put it in. Hence our last paragraph reads:

These policies and procedures are not exhaustive and will be modified and added to from time to time. All employees are expected to use common sense in all areas of their work responsibilities. If you have any questions, ALWAYS ask a manager or the owner.

Oh and by the way, I usually try not to use the words "*employees*" and "*common sense*" in the one sentence.

You will find a copy of our Policy and Procedure Manual at www.hopelesstohero.com.

Chapter 10   Provide Effective Discipline

Most of us would like to think that there would never come a time when we would have to impose some form of discipline in the workplace, and in particular, *our* workplace. This element of your interaction with your employees, although not the most pleasant, is an essential part of the employer/employee relationship.

No reasonable employer is thinking about the process of letting people go when he interviews or trains new personnel. That being said, you must have a framework in place as to how you will discipline your people, if, not *when*, the situation arises. Your framework starts with your Policy and Procedure or Employee Manual. As mentioned in the previous chapter, if you do not have your guidelines firmly in place, it becomes very hard to police them.

It would be like trying to police traffic regulations without having any laws in place. What do you get when this is the scenario? Chaos, pandemonium and anarchy. You would have the patients running the asylum. Hence, discipline should be one of the key focal points of your manual and your employees should be well aware of the consequences of any breaches of policy.

The Standard

Most areas in the United States and other countries adhere to some form of an "employment at-will" policy. This simply means that apart from specific contractual agreements, an employer can dismiss any employee for any reason, as long as it is not illegal or discriminatory. This can be done on the spot with no warning or two-week notice. Employees under a similar banner can resign without giving their two-week notice. This is also called a "right to work" law.

Now because you have the power to do this does not mean than you do not keep proper and accurate records as to employees' actions that warrant the termination of their employment. Employee records need to be updated regularly with entries as to their experience, training and any discussions or disciplinary based actions. Regardless of what kind of business you own or what kind of product or service you provide, most employers have adopted a generic *"three strikes and you're out"* policy. This is a relatively easy, common sense, and coverall policy that applies to most circumstances in the work place. It is comprised of the following three steps:

➤ First offence - Verbal warning (also recording in your employee file)
➤ Second offence - Written warning (filed in the employee file)
➤ Third offence – "On your way – Sunshine"

This obviously is dependent on the severity of the incident that has necessitated the disciplinary response. In one of our locations, a male employee dropped a very audible "F Bomb" in the back of the store during our after school rush. No three strikes here—we elevated our response straight to the third strike and showed him the door.

This process works well in most scenarios, however you have two very important points to consider—what the law requires of you and the severity of the offence.

Know the Law - *Again*

I can't reiterate this point enough and I won't go through the process too deeply again here as the core of the principle of this has been dealt with in chapter 3. You have to know your bounds and limitations so far as discipline is concerned with your local statutes. Laws can even be different for adults and minors in the same workplace, so you cannot take a "one punishment fits all" approach, as *you* may find yourself on the wrong end of a "smacked bottom," figuratively speaking. And by the way, I think you will find "smacked bottoms" as a form of discipline will be against labor laws in most municipalities; just sayin!

Level of Response

This is where there is some flexibility in your response to a breach of your workplace policy and procedure. Flexibility here can be your best friend or your worst nightmare, so you should be very familiar with what constitutes a breach of your business policy and what would be an appropriate level of response.

I first learned of this principle as a police officer. In the police academy, we were shown a diagram to illustrate how to mete the appropriate "use of force" response for any given situation. It was called the "Use of Force Wheel."

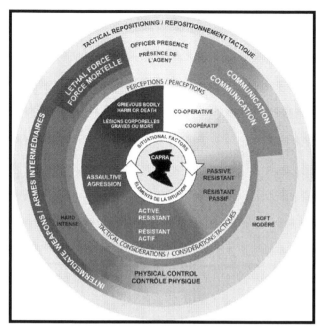

Use of Force Wheel – Royal Canadian Mounted Police

This diagram helps police officers identify escalating levels of threat and allows them to study an appropriate response that neutralizes the threat without stepping over the line of the "use of force" policy. You can see that as the level of threat increases, so does the response.

Now I am not advocating that a similar "use of force" should be used in the workplace, but the principle is a very powerful one. May I suggest that you should have a similar system in regards to your disciplinary process for your business. You should have a category of breaches where a simple "talking to" may be appropriate. In other instances you may move straight to a more dramatic but effective level of discipline, as demonstrated with our back room "F Bomber."

When employees are suitably informed of the consequences of their actions, it makes disciplinary action in the workplace much easier to accomplish. With such a diagram available to your employees, you should never hear an "I didn't know" or "Nobody told me" comment ever again.

Just Because You Can Doesn't Mean You Should

Beware not to have some kind of knee-jerk reaction and take disciplinary measures before you find out the motivation or root of an employee's actions. In most scenarios discretion can be the better part of valor and taking time to investigate a certain situation may shed light on a matter that may make you think differently about your response. One of our assistant managers started to come in late for work regularly and began to be consistently overanxious and tense. This employee was always one of our most trusted and reliable hires so this behavior seemed a little out of the ordinary.

Rather than imposing some kind of disciplinary action, I took the time to ask her what was going on in her life. As it turns out she was slowly but surely becoming a victim of domestic violence in her relationship with her boyfriend. Although her actions constituted a breach of our policy manual, we chose to become more involved to help her remedy her personal situation.

Over the period of three or four weeks, I gave her counsel as an ex-policeman to take certain steps to ensure that the cycle of violence was broken. Unfortunately, after weeks of working with her, she still did not have the motivation to change her personal circumstances and it was affecting both her work and those who were working around her.

Late one evening on a closing shift, her boyfriend came to the store and tipped over tables and chairs in a fit of rage. This was a circumstance that could not be accepted in the workplace, and I gave her an ultimatum. Her relationship and the subsequent violence needed to change or I could not have her work in the store anymore. Unfortunately she chose to leave and remain in this toxic union which disappointed me more than anything. Not only did I lose an excellent employee, I was afraid she was in a situation where she could lose so much more.

This story did have a happy ending however and six months later I came across her while shopping. She had dumped the loser, had her life back together again and I was more than happy to have her come back and work for us once more. There is generally a root cause or event that leads to someone breaching or not complying with your policy and procedures. It can be beyond an employee's control or sometimes it is just complacency or arrogance. It may be lack of motivation or a feeling of self-righteousness.

In most cases, minor infractions can be dealt with at the lower level of escalation. Let's say sixteen-year-old Lucy is a part time worker in your business and after a month or so she starts to come in late for most of her shifts. Not only is this not a good employee practice, but it puts pressure on other employees who are covering for her or preventing someone from going home who is finishing their shift.

Time for a Chat
Now before you launch into a tirade that Attila the Hun would be proud of, remember again, there may be legitimate or personal reasons for tardiness. Perhaps there is trouble at home, or a close

personal friend has been diagnosed with a severe illness. Always ask the reason for the tardiness first.

"Hey, Lucy, I noticed you have been late for work a lot lately. Is everything all right?" If you don't hear about Aunt Fannie's kidney stones or any other dire personal issues, you have discharged your humanitarian duties, and now on to the matter at hand.

"Well being late not only puts pressure on the rest of us, it's not a good habit to be in. Remember our policy is to be here at work and ready to serve customers at your shift start time. I really need you to improve in this area. I am going to make a note in your file that we spoke about this, and hopefully that will be the last of it. Do you have any questions? OK Thanks."

A key point here is to identify the section of the handbook that is being breached and have her acknowledge that she is aware of it. She should be, as you had her sign a copy of her acceptance of these guidelines in her personal file. Once she slinks back to the counter, make sure you do what you said you were going to do and make a note in her file: Time, date, place and topic of conversation. This simple act has saved an employer's backside more than once or twice.

Well, Lucy recovers well for a couple of weeks and then falls back into her tardy slump again. Now it is time for some written notice. *"Hey, Lucy, we have spoken before about your being late. Have circumstances changed or are we just picking up some bad habits?"* Again—when there is no legitimate reason for the behavior, you hand her a note written or printed on company letterhead and say, *"Here is a written warning. I can't run my business effectively when you are coming in late. Please understand that next time we talk about this, I will have to let you go."*

She swears on her grandmother's stones it will not happen again and returns to work. Two weeks later we are back to the same routine and you have no alternative but to let her go. Again, be very aware of your responsibilities and rights as an employer and acknowledge hers rights also.

Again, make copious notes because as soon as she gets home, your phone is going to ring—and it's not Lucy on the other end. It is Mom or Dad wanting to know why you made their little angel cry. Having notes here is the ultimate vindication, and reading through her employee file (if you are permitted to by law) will easily justify your actions. You may be limited to simply stating that it is a matter between her and her employer and you are not permitted to explain any further. Even if this is the case, a well-documented event log in Lucy's file will protect you against any future questions or complaints.

In closing, here are a few more points you may find helpful.

Be Friendly but Not Their Friend
When our daughter Emily was about five years old, she started addressing us not by our usual titles of Mom and Dad but by our first names of Stephen and Caroline.

We thought it was cute for the first couple of days. *"Stephen, can you get me a drink?" "Caroline, can we go to McDonald's?"* However after a short time, we noticed a strange phenomenon taking place. Soon our five-year-old was not only refusing our parental requests but commenced telling us what to do around the house. We had an urgent parental council meeting. This was back before the days of Dr. Phil when we had to work these issues out by ourselves.

My wife and I came to the conclusion that while Emily was addressing us by our first names, she felt she was on an equal playing field with us. We were no longer an authority figure in our home, but more like roommates, and hence, Emily felt she was no longer subordinate to us. As soon as we suggested that we be addressed by "Mom" and "Dad" again, we returned to the family bliss that we were used to.

Hence "Be Friendly but Not their Friend." As soon as your employees see you as an equal, you will lose all authority and sometimes respect in the workplace. There is lot to be said for the mutual respect that an employer and employee have for one another's roles in the business. I'm not suggesting that the workplace needs to be a dull and solemn environment; in fact we have always strived to have exactly the opposite feeling in our stores. But there still needs to be that line.

Teach the Ability to "Take Instructions and Corrections"
I have that found in business and in life, there are two main elements to maintain any worthwhile relationship. These principles have particularly helped me in many situations with my employees' attitude and their willingness to work within the boundaries of our businesses policy and procedures.

I have simply explained at some point in an employee's initial training that if they are able to follow instructions and accept corrections and counsel, they will have a long and happy working relationship with their employers, supervisors and other workmates. Think about it. Is there any situation that cannot be resolved if an employee tried his or her best to follow instructions?

There will be times, whether by their fault or not, the task or job assigned is not completed or done correctly. In this situation, if this employee can put pride aside and take constructive criticism to change behavior or improve his output, there would never be the need for resolution in the workplace. This isn't an "I am right and you are wrong" scenario, or a need to be on a power trip as an employer or manager.

The fact of the matter is that there needs to be structure and leadership in any workplace for that business to grow and succeed. Employees who do not respect the authority of the owner or manager and cannot respond positively to these principles will continue to be a thorn in your side. If an employee cannot follow instructions or take correction or criticism, then what benefit are they to your business success?

The Attitude Test

Back in my old policing days, we used to have a very commonly used phrase called the "Attitude Test." Again, not a power issue at all, but if members of the public found themselves on the wrong side of the law, regardless of whether it was a stop sign violation or a more serious crime, things always went a little more smoothly for them if that passed the "Attitude test." I think this test has universal applications.

I am going to put my "Old Fogey" hat on here and suggest that as each generation grows up in a more technologically advanced environment, where the font of all wisdom and knowledge is in the palm of their hands, the level of personal respect for others seems to be waning.

Add to this the real fact that in most western societies, kids don't really *need* part time jobs anymore. We seem to have a very deep chasm between what employers expect from the employees and what employees are willing to submit to. If you recall some of the responses to my small business survey in the introduction to this work, nearly all of these issues are attitudinal or motivational based. Teaching employees to pass the Attitude Test early in their employment will save both yourself and them a load of grief.

The need for a solid framework of discipline within your business has never been more relevant. You also have to be aware that there can be no gray area or fuzzy lines when it comes to discipline. If you give an inch they will take a mile; if you leave the doorway open a crack, they will open it all the way.

The Ripple Effect

I have heard a few employers tell me that if I haven't fired someone every one or two months, I'm not doing my job as a manager. I think that mentality is ridiculous. Think of the time, effort and money you have tied up in the investment of these employees. And by all means you must understand that it is an investment. This time and effort when invested correctly, should gain you a high rate of return.

I do know however that when one person is fired, it sends

shockwaves through the rest of the employees. When one of the crew is "voted off the island," the remaining survivors always experience moments of introspective thinking which can write a listing ship in many cases. Unfortunately when one of the bad apples is let go, you start to hear comments like, *"I'm glad you let him go, he was robbing you blind for months."*

Great—thanks for the heads up.

Chapter 11   Uniformity

I am so passionate about employees looking and feeling their best that I decided to dedicate a whole chapter on this principle. Uniforms create a unique atmosphere and motivation not only for the employee but the customers as well. I will say it again:

You never get a second chance at a first impression.

When a customer, perhaps a first time customer to your business walks in the door and approaches the customer service area, they will judge the taste of your product or the effectiveness of your service based on what the person standing in front of them looks like. It may not be fair but it is the truth in the majority of instances.

If your representative is wearing a dirty or crumpled shirt, if they have dirt under their fingernails or chook's nest hairdo, a perception is formed in the mind of this customer. This perception may very well be that this is how you do business or how your products are going to taste.

Remember, the individual's perception is their reality. Now imagine that same scenario with an employee who had washed and ironed her uniform before coming to work, has her hair neatly done and tucked under a cap and all of a sudden, a different perception is gained by the customer.

Complacency Kills

When we opened our St. Louis, Missouri location, all of our employees were very excited about their new jobs and the buzz that the new shop created. Our uniforms were relatively unique and all eighteen of our initial crew looked great in their gear. Our uniform consisted of a Green Polo shirt that had our logo on the front, coupled with a white baseball cap and a yellow bar apron. Employees were requested to wear white knee length shorts, skirts or trousers.

That excitement changed over the long and drawn-out winter months and our employees contracted a little "cabin fever." Locked up in the shop with few customers in the down season took its toll. Shirts would come in crumpled and dirty, white shorts turned into brown shorts and even, heaven forbid—jeans! Hats and name badges were becoming a part time accessory rather than the full-time necessity.

It was time to pull out the old photo of our crew when we first opened. (Note the urban rapper standing next to yours truly in the back row busting a move.) The crisp, clean uniforms and the beaming smiles reminded them of their former selves and with that came a renewed commitment to look every part the model employee. Each crewmember remembered that little fire that burned within their bosom from the time we opened and committed to do a little...no...a lot better.

Uniforms Create Consistency and a Feeling of Teamwork

When I was in the Police Academy, we stood on parade every morning for six months to have our dress uniform and appearance judged by the staff sergeant, who seemed to have developed a penchant for picking on me. In particular, my skills in ironing (or lack thereof). If he didn't stop right in front of me, he would walk past me slowly, and just when I breathed a sigh of relief, he would quickly turn on his heel and double back. It was always the same corny line:

"CHRISTENSEN, WHAT DID YOU IRON THAT SHIRT WITH... A 4 IRON?"

Oh yes, the memories. I can laugh about it now, but the parade each morning was a virtual nightmare for me. A nightmare I decided to replicate for my disheveled employees on a regular basis.

We spent a lot of time and effort on our uniforms. You don't really have to spend a lot of money on uniforms, but we went the extra mile to make sure our staff looked the part. When one of the crew fronted up with a uniform that was less than our agreed standard, I was always ready with the statement, "What did you iron that shirt with? A 4 iron?" Yes, they looked at me with the same disdain I had felt for the staff sergeant many years ago, but it certainly got the message across loud and clear.

Name that Employee

Scott Ginsburg has an incredible story about a nametag that changed his life. Scott went to a meeting on his college campus, put a nametag sticker on and inadvertently left it on for the rest of the day. As he walked around campus, he found people much more engaging and friendly and attributed it to this sticky name simply stating, "Hello. My Name is Scott."

Ginsburg built an entire customer service industry around this seemingly minor event. He has worn that nametag (or a replacement of it) for over five thousand days earning a spot in the Ripley's Hall of Fame. He even has a tattoo of it on his chest in case he misplaces it. Scott speaks at events and had published numerous books and articles on the process of building loyalty through customer interaction.

You can find out more at www.hellomynameisscott.com.

His main angle is the relationship that builds with the simple exchange of names can form relationships and introduce opportunities that may never have happened if both or all parties continued to remain anonymous.

You would be surprised how the relatively minor expense of a simple nametag will result in a much more committed crew and an increasingly loyal customer base. When customers engage with your employees by name, it elevates the customer service relationship. That guy who serves up your plate of fish and chips or who girl who takes your money at the register is no longer a nameless face. They are now Jared and Emily.

When customers engage with your crew by name, there is a social interaction that transcends the financial transaction. They now become associates, perhaps even friends. This concept plays a huge part in the loyalty a customer has to your business. Remember the classic sitcom *Cheers*, set in a downstairs bar. Customers like Norm and Cliff became characters and regular fixtures, because there was a real connection between the owners, employees and customers.

For this reason, all of our employees were required to wear nametags. They were simple yellow badges that I purchased at a trophy store and had their name placed on them with a printed clear sticker. The policy was that nametags were to be left in the drawer at the store when they went home, but more often than not, tired employees would stumble out the door with and not return the tag. For this reason we had a couple of "I Forgot my Nametag" nametags.

It was a tongue in cheek lesson taught and amazingly, our customers would get a real kick out of seeing one of the employees (usually a male) wearing one of these tags. Sometimes I think the guys would wear it as a badge of honor in recognition of their spirit of rebellion. As elementary as this principle is, nametags will make a subtle but long lasting impression on both your employees and your customers.

The Dos and Don'ts of uniforms.

Now I am going to throw a disclaimer in here. You may be already doing some of the "*dos*" so to speak, and if so, congratulations. You also might be participating in some of the "don'ts" behavior. Don't take umbrage at your humble correspondent for picking your concept to death. *You* need to make the decisions as to what the uniform policy will be in your store and stick to your guns. I think you will find, though, deep down in your heart of hearts, that I am probably right. Just sayin!

Do:

Take a cue from the national brands. You may not want to have a hundred locations. You may not even want ten, you may be happy with the singular location that is doing well for you. Regardless, you have to admit that the national and regional brands in your business sphere have probably spent millions of dollars in research and development of what their customers respond to in relation to the look of the crew. What they execute so far as their employee uniforms are concerned probably makes good business sense.

Don't:

Think that the national brands really don't have anything to do with your humble business and the clientele you are seeking. The truth of the matter is that most consumers would rather support local than the national chains (even though in most markets it is a "local" businessman who is operating the concept). If you can provide a quality product, the value that goes along with it and a great looking and engaging crew, you are steps ahead of the competition.

Do:

Some research as to what level and length of clothing is acceptable in your market. Generally, the conservative business casual is the norm and well accepted across all spectrums of customer bases.

Don't:

Settle for jeans. I know, I know—I am going to have a lot of haters here but "Haters gonna hate." You don't see national brands allowing their employees to wear jeans. The reason is that there is no uniformity to the term "jeans"—blue, dark blue, stone wash, acid wash, skinny, mom and butt hangers just to name a few. I know it's easy, convenient and everybody owns a pair, but once we allow convenience to dictate how our employees look, you open the door to booty shorts, wife beaters, shoulder pads, leg warmers and a slew of other types of apparel that you yourself probably wouldn't be caught dead in.

Do:

Provide the crew with the amount of uniform items they need. Regular crewmembers who work once or twice a week may be issued one uniform shirt, one cap and an apron. Crewmembers such as managers or full time employees should receive more to assist them in looking fresh and clean for every shift.

Don't:

Assume that just because you have provided a newly designed and clean uniform that they will wear it as you intended. You must give instructions as to how the uniform should be worn. E.g., Caps must not be worn backwards or to the side. No long-sleeved privately owned t-shirt should be worn under the uniform shirt—that kind of thing. These guys will always find a way to take what you have given them and tweak it to the so-called fashion of the day.

Do:

Have spare uniform items in case of emergency. In our line of work, a chocolate shake explosion will instantly render a clean uniform shirt unwearable for the rest of the shift. Having spares will avoid your crew spending a couple of wet and sticky hours behind the counter.

Don't:

Give these items out willy-nilly. Depending on where you get your kit from, I would imagine there will be some cost to the process. Giving the crew the impression that they can just go and grab another shirt or cap from the back without being accountable or signing for it opens the door for your unscrupulous employees to select a couple of rad outfits for the party they are going to this weekend.

Do:

Use your uniform to build your brand. The design of your uniform doesn't need to be elaborate or expensive. You may have a simple printed t-shirt or a plain colored polo shirt under a contrasting colored apron with your logo on it. Regardless of the combination, this is a chance to put your name and logo in front of your customers, so take the opportunity to do it well. A lot of small businesses actually sell their uniform shirt or branded apparel with great success. Nana's Frozen Custard in Hixson, Tennessee came up with the tagline "Who's Your Nana" and emblazoned it over the back of a brightly colored tie-dyed shirt. Retail sales went through the roof and a community's new catch cry was "Who's your Nana."

Don't:

Let your employees use this "brand building" opportunity to wear their uniforms outside of work hours. Any negative behavior or incidents that happen while your employees are wearing their uniform outside of work hours can have a direct correlation back to your business. Our employees are told they can wear their uniform to work and back home again. That's it. McDonald's in Australia follows this principle so closely that they used to require all employees to cover up their uniform before leaving the premises at the end of their shift.

Send a Clear Message

In closing, these are principles that your employees must have a core knowledge of. When they wear your uniforms, they are an extension of your business and become your personal representative. Any press or publicity, even if it is just in the mind or impression of the consumer can make or break your brand equity.

Let me give you a couple of memorable examples.

Our urban rapper loved to tweak his uniform to fit with the swag he had collected to much expense over the years. The baseball cap found its way to a thirty-five-degree angle and the white trousers started to slip lower and lower down his backside. I guess I can understand some of the crazy fashion trends over the years, but this whole saggy trousers hanging down the backside and held in place at the top of the thighs with a tight belt makes no sense to me.

In any case, we instituted a special policy for him. "Low Pants No Chance." If the belt line was any lower than his waist, he would have no chance of working in our business. I even caught him a couple of times sauntering from the parking lot to the front door, and I would mouth the words "Low Pant No Chance" through the front window which would result in an immediate vertical lift reaction.

Another memorable instance of an employee getting on the wrong end of the uniform policy got the young man sent home. Alex was a great employee with an engaging personality and very reliable. He didn't show the same passion for ironing. I had dropped the "4 Iron" line on him a couple of times but this only instituted short-term change. One afternoon he came into work and was about to sign into the register when I stopped him.

"Hey, Alex. You can't show up to work looking like that."
"Looking like what?"
"I don't understand how you can get a shirt that wrinkled. It looks like you washed it, wrung it into a tight ball when it was still wet, put it on the bottom of a pillowcase and swung it around your head till it dried like that."

He smiled and went to type his employee number into the register.

"I'm serious. You've got to go home and iron that shirt."
"But I am just about to start my shift."
"Well you'd better be quick."

He slowly walked to the front door and gave one me one more look to see if I was just joking around. I motioned him with my hand *"Go on."*

He returned to the store about fifteen minutes later.

"Now that's what I am talking about."

He fake-smiled and proceeded to log in for the shift. Now I am sure word spread around the crew that I had lost my marbles, but no doubt the message was also sent loud and clear. You cannot show up to work looking substandard and expect to work at your peak performance or earn your customers' respect.

If you want to have super employees, you have to give them a super hero outfit and expect it to be fitting of their super hero customer service powers.

Chapter 12   Training and Opening Days

For most small business, staff training usually runs by the "feast or famine" program. When you are going through your initial startup, there is no end to the training programs you put your help through. POS training, customer service training, coffee training and so on and so forth. It seems a shame that the restaurant owner doesn't go through "Training Training" prior to this point so he can foresee and perhaps prevent a potential information overload on his prospective staff members.

These initial training sessions can be a high stress couple of days where employees, who for the most part are new to your systems, products and services, are participating in rapid learning sessions on equipment, policy and standard operating procedures. It is of the utmost importance that you keep an eye on the progress of each of your hires here. You do not want to imply that this will be the general stress level in your business.

Here are some tips that have always worked for me in the hundreds of initial training sessions I have been involved in.

Have an Agenda

This sounds like common sense however, you may be surprised as to how many business owners have a rough draft in their head of what needs to be covered, which leaves room for items and important information to be left out. May I suggest the following?

> ➢ Welcomes and introductions
> ➢ Your story and why you are going into this business
> ➢ A history or story of how the business came to be

- Policy and Procedure manual (have them sign the final page to show they fully understand the contents)
- Job description and general shift requirements
- Menu, product or service review
- Equipment training
- Portion control (if in the food industry)
- Register and customer service techniques
- Closing session and general questions

You may need to have two sessions to cover this information. I have found that a couple of three or four-hour sessions will suffice but be prepared that some of the crew may not be able to make both. This is also paid training so everyone is to be prepared and ready to take this information in.

You may have them attend the first session in general civilian clothing and then the second session they will be in full uniform. If you have the uniform policy in your policy and procedure handbook, they should be well aware of the requirements.

Decide Whether All Staff Members Need Training in a Particular Area

If only a small percentage of staff members (perhaps supervisors) will be using the POS system to close off at the end of each shift, only have them attend the more rigorous training on the system. The up and coming supervisors can learn from those who have already mastered the art down the track. There is no point in having the kitchen crew learn about the functions of the security system when they will be long gone by the time the alarm needs to be turned on at the end of the day's trade.

Plan and Space out Training Days.

Usually by the time the staff training is scheduled to happen, so is everything else. Tiles are going into the bathroom, the ceiling is being wired for internet and music speakers and the walk-in cooler is being installed. With all of this commotion in and around you while you train, it is no wonder only half of what you say is ever digested. Between the staff being repulsed by the old guy with the baggy shorts at the top of the ladder installing cable and you being dragged away every fifteen minutes to make on-the-spot decisions, these guys don't stand half a chance of learning.

Always ensure that you have a couple of good sessions and are uninterrupted with other tasks pulling you every which way.

Try and Ease into the Process

If you decide that the most effective and quiet time to conduct a training seminar in early on a Saturday morning, bring out the griddle and flip some pancakes for breakfast. Or order in some pizza and drinks for the break. Remember, this will be one of the first glimpses they see you wearing your boss hat. You don't want to have these guys think their potential boss will always be the stress monger you are exhibiting in the opening phase of your business.

Don't Try and Do It All Yourself

Sure you know how to make good coffee, and there may be many good reasons why you will want to train the staff on how to make a perfect cappuccino, but do you not remember that the coffee machine rep said he would train your staff as part of your package? Its not all about you being the holder of all knowledge. In fact, it would do you good to stand at the back and get a refresher course yourself.

Always ask a potential supplier of equipment whether they will include training as well as being at your opening day as part of the package. They should be the experts in their field.

Communication Is the Key

Can I suggest the worst staff/customer communication we have all experienced? Have you have pulled up at the gas station and proceeded to fill your tank, when the attendant inside grasps the microphone to advise you to pay for your purchase inside? Mostly what is heard is an incoherent mumble over the speakers, which leaves you wondering who this person is talking to and what exactly did they say.

Making sure your communication is clear and concise will always make your trainings more effective. Also having a handout for all of the items you are going to cover will also be very helpful and it is something they can take home and reread after the excitement of the day.

Open Communication Channels

There may be some issues that some employees will want to talk to you about privately rather than in front of the group. Giving out your contact details at the end of the training is important. Each employee should have the ability to contact you directly with any concerns or complaints.

Family and Friends Night

If you are in the opening stages of a retail business, I would definitely recommend an open night, or a family and friends night before you open. This is an event where the business is on full dress rehearsal, your product is prepped and ready to go, and your crew looks great in their freshly cleaned and pressed uniforms. The registers are in training mode and you are ready for your first night's business—well customers anyway. This is an evening where you are introducing your product or service to the community, family and friends for free as a last precursory wave of operations before opening your doors for real. This is important for a number of reasons.

This is your first real marketing opportunity.

Family and friends who helped you through the business startup process are definitely welcome on your guest list as well as the immediate family of your employees. Their attendance shows support for their son or daughter, mom or dad.

However, you should definitely use this opportunity to invite pivotal community members and the press for a preview of your business. Remember to think of those who hold communication keys in your community—school teachers and principals, hairdressers, police and fire chiefs, pastors and ministers all are well respected and community focal points.

One business owner used a whole week to conduct his training. On Monday at lunchtime, he had teachers, principals and teachers' aids from schools all over his area attend for free ice cream. Tuesday was the local car salesman, hairdressers and other prominent "talkers" in the community. Wednesday was emergency services and local city leaders and so on. What a great way to train your crew and get significant promotional activity at the same time.

Your employees will actually see how busy your business may get.
It's all fun and games while the crew is getting to know each other in the first couple of training sessions, but when the door is open on your family and friends night, and the line is out the front door, things can change in the psyche for these guys. For some employees this is a make-or-break situation. Believe it or not, I have had three employees resign on family and friends night claiming that they could not handle the stress of the situation; and no, I wasn't disappointed. I would much rather find out that the stress tolerance level was low on an employee that night than our first or second night live.

You get to meet the parents of teen workers.
This is more beneficial for the parents than it is for you. Moms and dads like to meet the man or woman their little ones are reporting to and working for on a weekly basis. It is good relations to "press the flesh." Give them a business card and inform them that you are more than happy to have them contact you if they have any concerns. You obviously don't really mean that. The last thing you want is anxious parents calling you because their precious little Timmy chipped a nail while cleaning the storeroom; however, it is kind of obligatory on your part.

Most importantly, you get to see your business in operation.
Take some time to stand back and watch the process of how the customers are flowing, how your employees are reacting to the incoming orders and how they process them. You may find that you have trash cans too far away from cutting stations or some of your

equipment is too close together on the counter. Customers may not flow in the order and pick process like you thought they would.

These are all very important observations to take note of before you go live, so through the greetings and salutations of the evening, be sure to take some private time to watch the operation, take notes and give yourself time to make some changes before your opening day.

When It's Live, It Gets Real
When you are formulating and executing your initial training for your business, you will find it is an exciting and enjoyable time for both you and your employees. The store around you has come together and your product or service is available and ready to be trained with.

I know from my perspective with retail ice cream, our initial training for employees is an exciting time where the kids can't wait to get their hands on some freshly made ice cream, hot fudge and lashings of whipped cream and so forth.   It is at this time that you will need to instill in your crew that things are entirely different when honest to goodness, real living, breathing and paying customers are standing before you with their hard-earned dollars in their hands.

Suddenly the training they enjoyed with their coworkers standing before them as mock customers seems like a walk in the park. Some new employees who seemed to perform very well in training can sometimes struggle when things are "live."

Live Ammo vs. Blanks

The most intense portion of training at a police academy is the firearms training. Many applicants, including myself, had never held, loaded or fired a hand gun before, which added to the tension.

Firearm training was held at the academy range (both indoor and outdoor) and consisted of written examinations, drills, working with blank ammunition and finally live rounds—in that order. I remember as the weeks rolled on most of us became impatient to get some live ammo "up the chamber" so to speak. Written exams were tedious and boring, and constant drills in assembling and dissembling our handguns grew to be monotonous. When we finally moved up to working with blank rounds, we had a little more excitement, however many in our academy class kept asking when the real bullets would be introduced.

I remember very intently, the day that our instructors wheeled out multiple carts loaded with green ammunition boxes. We were asked to gather round as the lids were popped open and hundreds of the bright shiny brass shells of live ammunition came into view. The excitement that we all anticipated was absent. There was just silence. Suddenly all of this just became real. Very real.

We discovered that when our exams, drills and dry firing were over, we were confronted with the very real responsibility to use our tools in a live environment where mistakes mattered. I think you get the analogy here, and although you may not be dealing with life and death mistakes, your crew needs to appreciate that the training you are providing them can be the difference between the life and death or your business and their jobs.

Many employees, like many young police cadets, can be overawed by the very real situation of going "live." Serving and confronting paying, sometimes problematic or complaining customers can be overwhelming, particularly for younger employees.

These principles need to be conveyed to your crew for their benefit. You also need to beware that some employees who cruise through training day may react very differently in live customer interactions and may need further time or training to help them keep up with your expectations.

Soft Openings

A couple of tips on benefitting from your training agenda.

When you have your crew thoroughly trained, your "family and friends" night and the lessons learned are behind you, you can lock in your opening day. Believe me when I tell you that you do not want to open on a Friday, Saturday or Sunday. These are the biggest retail days of the week and your head will blow clean off your shoulders. A soft opening is taking the opportunity to open your business on a Monday, Tuesday or Wednesday rather than a monster retail day. Save that for your grand opening.

On a soft opening day, you will grow with the trickle and then increasing flow of customers until your first weekend day of trade when you will be at least somewhat physically and emotionally prepared to provide your customers' needs with the best product or service without being overwhelmed. Please do not be concerned that no one will come in on your first day of business, which would be utterly demoralizing. During your build out, construction and training time frames, you will be constantly interrupted by potential customers asking when you will open. Another good idea is to have a suction cupped brochure holder on the front door with a brief flyer on your opening hours and when you will be open.

One of our store openings was delayed because of a building department inspection that dragged on and on, and some minor construction work needed to be completed. By the time I had certificate in hand and permission to open, it was 4:45 p.m. on the Friday of Labor Day weekend in the US. My employees looked at me wondering whether I was going to take my own advice and wait till Monday or swing open the doors and "have a go" as the Aussies say. I chose the latter. What could go wrong, right? I am the ice cream bloke after all; I had helped open over five hundred retail ice cream and food business by this stage and felt fully confident in my ability to not follow my own advice. Boy.

Within fifteen minutes up lighting up the Open signs, there was a line out of the front door and the registers were humming. Two of our employees were in the back room having a nervous breakdown, and to tell you the truth, while my fingers were scrambling all over the register to locate menu item buttons, there was a little tear trickling down my cheek. It's not worth the stress and the poor first impression your customers will get. It is worth the wait to open on your own terms on a day of the week that will ease you in.

Chapter 13   Teaching Effective Customer Service

Working from a home office means there are often errands that need to be run to the post office and UPS store and other local supportive businesses. From my home I am almost exactly between two UPS stores. Both of them are about four miles from my front door and funnily enough, both are located in a grocery shopping mall. In fact both sites are almost identical. What happens inside, however, is a totally different story.

One of these locations was run by two brothers. Although they were adults, they reminded me of how I taunted and harassed my brother who was four years younger than me back when we were kids. Some days they would be back of the store yelling or arguing with each other. Other days they would be throwing rolls of bubble wrap around the back of the room. Although it was always entertaining, the customer service there was terrible. It always took me longer to accomplish any postage related activity there than at any other location.

The final straw was the half-filled bowl of mini Tootsie Rolls they had on the counter. In my humble opinion, a bowl of mini Tootsie Rolls is a nonverbal announcement to your customers that they are only worth the smallest and most inexpensive candy you can find.

The other UPS store was a different story. It was run by a husband and wife team who were always at the front counter and always engaging to their customers. Sure, they got to know their customers by names by virtue of the fact that they were a postage facility, but they seemed to go the extra mile in remembering each customer and engaging on a personal level. I was out of town once and needed something sent to me urgently. After calling the store, they comforted me by telling me to have my wife drop off the article to the location and they would handle the rest.

I felt as if the owners of this business really cared, not only about my postage needs, but about my needs personally.

On one occasion I was waiting in line and overheard a conversation at the front counter. The customer was telling of an incident that she experienced going to the old "Brothers Grimm" UPS location down the road. I think I overheard the words *"they were throwing packing peanuts at each other"* somewhere in the conversation.

Needless to say, I continued to patronize the second UPS location for many years. I was not the biggest customer they had, but imagine all of the smaller customers like myself who had been turned off one location and turned onto another. That collectively is a big shot in to the arm of any small business.

Why Kids Don't Get It

Cell phones and mobile devices have really changed the dynamic of communication of our youth today. Text, Facebook messaging, tweets, Instagram and other nonverbal communications have become so commonplace that it is not unusual to communicate electronically with family members within the walls of your own home without even moving off the couch or bed.

Back when I was a youngster running around Primrose Street with my brother and the other local yahoos, my dad would stand on the front porch and call our names through the neighborhood until we came in to wash up and have dinner. Although this experience was not always welcoming, I knew through the tone of my father's voice whether he was angry, happy or simply trying to get our attention. Now with electronic communication it seems that the interpersonal elements and nuances of communication have been almost eliminated.

Families sit around the lounge room, or even worse, the dinner table, typing away on tiny keyboards to friends and associates all around the world, or even worse, to each other sitting at the table! This is why I firmly believe that aliens and other species from more advanced civilizations look the way that they do.

Mouths are smaller because "nonverbal" has become the main channel of communication. They just don't use them much anymore. Eyes are bigger and rounder to look at tiny screens and fingers are elongated to type more efficiently on tiny keyboards. You know I am right. Well, maybe I am stretching things a little here but you get my point. Let's put down the phones for a little while and concentrate on the art of "face to face" communication.

I could have made this topic a sub section of your training day chapter. However, I honestly feel that this concept of customer service training deserves some separate attention.

It is the crux of a successful business and one of the reasons why people will return and tell their friends and associates about your business. Remember the three "En's."

1. End product
2. Environment
3. *Engagement*

When you are going through the process of selecting employees, this principle of engagement must be foremost in your mind. You need to be asking yourself of each potential hire, "Is this person going to be able to excel in making the customer feel appreciated and welcome?"

It is for this reason that I formulated the A E I O and U of Customer service.

The A E I O U of Customer Service

Great customer service is one of the three essential elements to make any retail store successful. Nothing is as refreshing as a friendly smile and a warm greeting when you walk into a business. Now I think we can all relate to an overfriendly experience where a sales associates was doing the equivalent of holding onto our leg while we walked around the store.

You need to teach your customer service team (and by the way that's a good term for them) the most effective way to give your customers a pleasant and enjoyable experience before they even get to taste any of your product or experience your service.. For this reason I have always stressed excellence in customer service in all of my training and education seminars. Excellence in customer service is one of the three main elements of our mission statement.

Mr. C's Ice Cream Emporium will provide its customers with a unique Ice Cream experience based on:

Value, Quality and Presentation of Product,
Excellence in Customer Service and a
Clean Fun and Entertaining Atmosphere.

So what is an effective way to teach some very basic and underlying principles of great customer service to our front line? I have developed a five step process that will help employees understand and remember the elements of customer service excellence. The A E I O and U

A Is for Acknowledgment
It's not always convenient to greet a customer verbally when they walk in the door although it is extremely important that we acknowledge their presence. Acknowledging a customer's entry into our business validates their visit almost immediately. We may be serving customers or scooping a cone or even talking on the phone, but we can still acknowledge a customer who walks in the door.

Sometimes it may be with a smile or a raised eyebrow to acknowledge their entrance. A very successful burger concept in the United States is Five Guys Burgers and Fries. Whenever you enter a Five Guys location, they don't always immediately greet you individually but they do call out how many people have just walked in the door. *"Three in the door."*

I'm sure this is for logistical or employee assistance reasons but when my wife and I enter a location and someone calls out *"two in the door"* at least I know that someone else knows that I am there and ready to place an order. Another great example of this principle is Highway 55 Burgers, Shakes and Fries. I spent many months working with the executive team of Highway 55, and each of them gets the importance of not only giving the customer a great experience culinarily but making them feel welcome as well.

Whenever you walk into any Highway 55 location, every employee in the place greets you with a cheery southern "How y'all doin?" And I mean everyone—the servers, the drive through team, the grill team, the guy mopping the floor—everyone. I have never been into a Highway 55 location anywhere and not felt appreciated and welcomed.

The opposite of this was recently demonstrated in a banking company commercial on television. In the Ally Bank commercial, a mock dry cleaner business was set up with a blender sitting on the counter. In front of the blender read a sign "Use blender for Service."

Hidden camera video showed customer after customer coming into the store and becoming increasingly frustrated with the lack of face to face communication. Some flicked the blender on and off. Others simply called out to the rear of the business hoping that someone would come to the rescue. A dramatic, yet effective, way of illustrating the need for acknowledgment and interpersonal communication.

E Is for Eye Contact

Eye contact is another essential part of the customer service experience. For some of your younger employees, this may feel awkward and uncomfortable considering the mainstay of communication in this generation is "eyes on a screen" rather than eyes on each other. Teaching employees to make good eye contact when greeting them is a staple for good communication, not only in the store environment but for life in general.

Making eye contact with customers helps them feel like you are engaging them personally and are attentive to their specific needs rather than just calling out a welcome into thin air and hoping someone will claim it as their own personal greeting. A very recent development in interpersonal communication is the science of Mirror Neurons. Mirror Neurons seated within our brains give us the ability to feel empathy, judge certain situations and respond appropriately to others' emotional needs and wants.

These neurons are triggered predominantly through what we see, particularly as we make eye contact with another. This is the basis for "Emotional Intelligence," or the ability to discriminate between others emotions, to evaluate them and respond accordingly to guide thinking and behavior. The amount of nonverbal information we process through our eyes is astounding. When we make eye contact with another, this process is doubled. It is an essential element of outstanding customer service.

I Is for Introduction

It is not uncommon for regional, national and International businesses, both retail and service, to have a script or formatted greeting as to how they want their customers to be engaged. A common denominator in all of these greetings is the introduction of the business name and the server's name. A welcome may go like this.

"Hi! Welcome to Mr. C's. My name is Julie. How can I help today?" At first your employees saying this greeting "word perfect" may seem contrived and insincere, however there is great wisdom in this three-step introduction.

Every time a customer hears your business name or sees your logo, it places a subconscious imprint in their mind about your business. If they hear it enough times, whenever they think ice cream, they will think "Mr. C's Ice Cream" because it has been said like that to them time and time again. A personal introduction that includes the crewmember's name also opens up a new level of interpersonal communication. Once customers know and greet your employees by name, there becomes a special bond between the crewmember and the customer.

Many business regulars know the employees by name and similarly crewmembers recognize customers, maybe not by their name but by what they order on a regular basis. Asking a customer if they would like their "usual" makes a customer feel as though their purchase and patronage to your business is remembered and important to the crewmember.

O Is for Observe

Once the customer has been acknowledged, eye contact has been made and your introduction has been delivered, observing the customer is the next most important thing. If the customer is ready to order and knows what they want, this process goes relatively quickly.

However if your customer seems to be confused or is roaming visually over the contents of your menu board, it is time to jump in with a suggestion or an offer to help. Customers generally will only read a menu board for about 106 seconds. There is a challenge here to not be overbearing but to observe to see if they are confused or perhaps need assistance in the ordering process. More on this in the next chapter.

Some of the confusion may come as a result of the layout of your menus or menu boards. Menus should be laid out, easily readable and preferably with photographs. Too much text or verbiage on a menu board can make these panels confusing and laborious to read.

U Is for Uniform

Not to belabor the point, but the way your crewmembers present themselves nonverbally says as much to your customer as what they speak to them. You don't have to spend a lot of money on uniforms, however, a uniform needs to be just that—uniform.

This means the same or consistent choice of apparel that is worn with a minimum standard of cleanliness and neatness. Just because everybody wears the same shirt, trousers or aprons doesn't mean there can be differing standards of dress. Uniform also applies to personal cleanliness and grooming. Long hair needs to be restrained and artificial nails, nail polish, dangly jewelry or multiple piercings can draw attention away from the uniformity of your employees.

Your customer will make an assumption on how you run your business and what your product or service will be like based on the experience they have with your customer service representative. Before they even have a sample they will more than likely make a judgment; and whether their judgment is correct or not, their perception is their truth.

"And...Action"

Another important principle is the actual training of how your employees greet, talk to and farewell your customers. The best way we achieved excellence in this area was through role playing.

We would have Sally be the Customer Service Officer, and John and Carly be the customers. John and Carly would walk outside and return arm in arm as mock customers. Sally commences her greeting. It was supposed to be a bright and cheery "Good Morning. Welcome to Mr. C's" but it sounded more like the mumblings of a lobotomy patient. I then took over the situation like that of a movie director.

"CUT, CUT, CUT! We need more emotion, more vibrancy, more connection. *Good Morning. Welcome to Mr. C's. How are you today?* Talk to the customer as if he is an old friend that you haven't seen for a long time. Now let's roll it again!"

Carly and John come in from outside again and Sally attempts another greeting. Her head rolls back and she stares into space somewhere out in the stratosphere. "Gud Mornin and welcome to Mr. C's."

"CUT, CUT, CUT! Sally, their eyes. Look at them in their eyes. Making eye contact with the customer gives you a connection and lets them know you are honest in your greeting. OK Let's Roll it Again!"

You get the picture. These youngsters will only get what you want them to say and do when you literally direct them in the way you want them to move. We have had employees so verbally challenged in this area that I had typed out the greeting and stuck in on the back of a straw box at the counter. "Guys, if you are really struggling with this greeting concept, just read the back of the straw box, for heaven's sake."

Making the process fun, but in the same vein, explaining exactly what you need your employees to say and do to your customers cannot be treated lightly. Great customer service is the key to unlocking the secret of return business and great word of mouth reviews.

Allow Your Customers To Give Feedback

The best feedback you will get regarding the effectiveness of your customer service processes are obviously...from your customers. I am amazed how many small businesses make this principle so hard for their customers to do.

Now granted I've been to many businesses where there is a customer service "How did we do?" form available near the register or some other prominent place. How many of us have been either extremely pleased or extremely disappointed in a service or product we purchased and just couldn't be bothered about filling out the form. Many consumers also want some form of anonymity during this process. Filling out a complaint form at the very counter where the alleged offence occurred, and for that matter, having the offender standing over you watching every pen stroke, really isn't a comfortable option for most consumers.

However, if your disgruntled customer can take a business card back to the office and type a quick email regarding their experience in the privacy of their own surroundings, I think you will get a better indication of the performance of your staff, both positive and negative.

May I suggest a simple business card with the owner / manager's name, email and phone number printed clearly and legibly? Place a cardholder in a prominent location with a small display worded to the effect of "We are interested in your feedback — please contact our manager with any comments." I think you will be surprised how many comments you will receive and how effective this tool will be in managing your staff members. Remember that these conversations are occurring already in cyber space on prominent social media and review sites.

Giving your customers an opportunity to vent to you or one of your managers may give the customer the "release" they needed, while averting a negative post on a page that will be out in the public forum for eternity.

Chapter 14   People Watching

Among my most favorite hobbies is that of people watching. Technically the term is described as "the observation of people and their interactions; usually without their express knowledge." Couple this activity with a dash of eavesdropping and you are in for a great afternoon's entertainment. And nowhere is there a more fascinating study of Homo sapiens in all of their social interactional glory than in the hub of airborne travel—the airport.

About sixty-six million people a year stream through London's Heathrow airport and that is nowhere close to the busiest in the world. Atlanta's Hartsfield-Jackson airport pumps through eighty-nine million passengers per annum. That's a whole lot of baggage—emotional and physical. The beauty of "airport" people watching is that every passenger not only has a story, but it's a story on the move.

There are multitudes of good reasons why we humans pack a bag and fly to destinations far and wide. Business, holidays, family visits and seeking treasure and adventure in a new land to name a few. Recently I did some serious people watching at the Milwaukee airport in Wisconsin.

This regional airport does not rank amongst the world's busiest, but with nine hundred thousand passengers a month streaming through; it's no hick town airport either.

As I got off my flight and walked from the concourse into the terminal, I was greeted with an unusual sight—a ping pong table

plonked right in the middle of the terminal, complete with bats and a ping pong ball.

As I walked past it, I was trying to determine whether it was a display for a sports store, or whether I could just pick up the bat and drum up some competition. As I was travelling alone, and didn't want to scare any little children, I decided to sit nearby, read a book and wait for my next flight. Every couple of minutes, I peered over the top of my pages and watched people walk by the table with the same bemused expression that I had exhibited, until a couple of boisterous Latino chaps, without hesitation scooped up the bats and launched into a ruthless battle—mano a mano.

It seemed as if they had lost track of where they were and pictured themselves in a game room in one of their basements, cheering with each victorious passing shot, and shouting in disappointment if they let a sitter through. At one point a small crowd even gathered with some small children clapping at the end of a long rally.

It really is fascinating to watch our fellow inhabitants in varying situations and standpoints. Learning to read the expressions and body language of people in different spheres not only provides some high quality entertainment, but it can also put you ahead of the curve in the retail business world as well.

Understanding Body Language

Sometimes our customers will say one thing, but their body language, posture or expressions may say something different. In some situations, our customers need not utter a single word; their nonverbal speech tells us volumes.

There are generally three situations where you will need to be aware of the customer's needs and wants:

1. The perusal of the menu
2. The wait for the order to be made or service to be completed
3. The response when they receive their product or service

As mentioned, studies have shown that most customers will read a menu for about 106 seconds before they make a decision, whether they have completed the menu not. This is important for you to know for a couple of reasons. The first of which is not to make your menu boards read like war and peace.

Over descriptive explanations of menu items and specials, no matter how eloquent or imaginative, can be problematic for a lot of customers. The effective use of photographs or images will greatly streamline and simplify the selection and ordering process.

Menu boards, regardless of what product or service you are selling should be "sectionized." This means grouping similar products or services together for ease of use, both for the customer and the employee who is serving them.

Secondly, you must train your employees to be aware if a customer is approaching the 106 time without ordering. Perhaps your menu is hard to read or filled with culinary goodness. Either way, after about thirty or forty seconds of silent reading, it's time for your employee to jump in with a friendly, "Have you been here before?" or "Can I help you make a selection?"

You may have a real money-spinner on the last panel of your menu board, and yet in most cases, your customer may never reach that point. Out of frustration, they may order something that is "safe" for them.

Most customers are happy to wait for their order to be filled. I say "most." It is not hard to read the body language of a customer who has waited past his patience, regardless of whether his frustration is justified or not. Moving from foot to foot, checking his watch or glaring at the staff member making the product are all telltale signs that something is brewing.

It is always a good practice to re-engage this customer, even, no, *especially* when his order is far from being completed. Customers want to feel acknowledged. Whether they have just walked into the shop, or whether they are waiting for their order. A simple "I will be with you shortly" or "It won't be too much longer sir, sorry for the wait" goes a long way to make molehills out of rapidly building mountains.

Lastly, it is just as important to read your customers' interactions when the product is handed over to them. For most employees, this is the point where they feel their work is done and they can move on to the next customer. No, no, no. The look on the customers' faces and their body language will continue to validate their feelings about what they ordered and what they received.

This is important because many dissatisfied customers won't mention a word of their disdain to you or your employees. Not even if you ask them.

But, they *will* tell friends, family and even total strangers about how you screwed up their order. Or how the caramel sundae they ordered had nuts on it when they distinctly said, "No nuts." The old adage about "Thrill a customer and they will tell ten people — Disappoint a customer and the will tell one hundred" is certainly true.

Again, in this day and age, this saying could not have more impact, as they are not just telling their friends, but also the entire universe. Social networking sites build communities around the food scene in many places. If you don't nab that small look of inquisitiveness or disappointment right there at the counter, you could pay for it through the eternities.

Chapter 15   Scheduling

Once your crew has been adequately trained, uniformed and prepped for all comers, you are responsible for creating the work roster. The roster, or schedule, is like your battle plan. You have a small army here that is equipped and ready to take on the challenge of all oncoming customers. (I guess you don't want to share this "military" analogy with the crew in case they see your customers as the enemy). This is human resource management at its finest—identifying the strengths and weaknesses of the resources you have at your disposal to create a plan to work effectively and efficiently in your business.

The roster has several elements to it:

- Identifying key employees to drive efficiency in peak times
- Keeping motivated employees teamed up with rookies
- Identifying talents or competencies and matching them with the shift requirements

A hastily thrown together employee schedule, or one that is simply replicated week after week, can be a huge source of demotivation in the workplace. This document is like the cherry on the top of your chocolate sundae. After all of the hard work you have done finding and training your employees, a well-constructed work schedule will have them humming like a well-oiled machine.

A Delicate Balance

In creating the roster, you have to balance effective coverage of personnel to take care of your customers' needs with the wants and needs of your employees' school and/or social lives. You also have to be very conscience of your labor costs and payroll percentage in adequately, but efficiently, staffing your business. This is a tough balance to achieve and many employers rack their brains in finding the perfect proportion of cost versus effective customer service.

Most employers sit down at the start of a week with a blank spreadsheet covering the assigned shifts for the upcoming roster and start combing through both the employee availability sheet and the request book.

For those of you who are very familiar with this process, you will no doubt testify to the struggle to fill all of your shifts with competent employees who are not only available but willing and able to work well on the shifts they are assigned. There is an art to pulling off a well-crafted roster that not only fills the shifts but does it effectively enough so that the personalities on that shift will have a cohesiveness and willingness to work together to achieve the elements of your mission statement.

Thankfully there are many tools to help this process become not only time efficient but almost enjoyable. Online programs that can be accessed virtually anywhere can be either free or subscription based and can trim down the time and anguish that most employers feel when tackling a new roster.

As the online support world is constantly changing with new programs and technologies available almost monthly, I have a full list of scheduling software and programs at www.hopelesstohero.com.

The program that we used the most is located at www.whentowork.com. This subscription-based program became such an asset to the management of our employees that it not only saved us time, it actually helped me manage the financial aspects of my business as well. In essence, you may need an hour or two to input employees' contact details, pay rates and other relevant information. Once this prep work is done, it is simply a matter of opening a new week, creating assigned shifts and clicking on an open shift. A drop down list appears with all of your employees' names and whether they are available for this shift or not.

It also lists the number of hours each employee has worked so far during the week and other helpful information to assist you in breezing through the schedule. Before posting or publishing the schedule, you have a reporting tab that will advise you on the total hours worked that week, what your payroll will be, and a plethora of other very useful information. Of course I do not receive any benefit from any business or company we recommend and as always, it is in your own best interest to look at the features and benefits of any program before signing up.

Here are some other tips to effective scheduling.

Staggering Shifts

Regardless of how effective your software or program is, it is not going to write the schedule itself. It is up to the employer or general manager to decide the times, duration and the overlapping or staggering of work shifts. Each individual shift is a small piece of the overall puzzle and how it interlocks or complements the others around them can either make or break the sense of motivation and effectiveness of the overall schedule.

Sometimes the number of employees to be placed on a certain shift or the overlap from one shift to another may not be overly apparent, however with some close attention to your sales per hour data, you should be able to get a clearer picture of your needs. This information should be available on your point of sale (POS) or register system. Using this data will help you staff and stagger shifts to get the maximum amount of manpower for the least amount of payroll. Let me give you an example:

Busy times in an ice cream shop are in the evenings. Not too many executives pick up a hot fudge sundae on the way to work in the morning. If I were to narrow that down some more, our key times for selling ice cream is between 7 p.m. and 9 p.m. at night. Having this knowledge means I need the greatest number of employees working during this two-hour period.

Split Shifts

Another challenge in the process of effective scheduling is giving the employees the hours they want while covering your needs as an employer. One effective way to accomplish this is to offer split shifts. This way an employee can work a two-hour shift (e.g. from 12 p.m. to 2 p.m.) and then come back for the remainder of their shift from 7 p.m. to 11 p.m. This not only helps you with coverage at the time that you need it, but also allows the employee to get the hours and pay that they need.

Again, you will have to check with state labor legislation to ensure that kind of system is approved.

Swapping Shifts

No employee schedule is set in stone and even the most meticulous attention to employees' needs will require tweaking while the roster is active. This may necessitate employees swapping or changing shifts from time to time. This is an area that requires some oversight. Remember that when you created the initial roster you were probably paying close attention to who was working with whom to create a synergy during that shift.

The synergy may end up way out of whack if John is teamed up with Michael, and everybody knows that when these two party animals get together, nothing is really accomplished. For this reason, many employers want (and probably need) to approve the swap. You may leave this responsibility to the General Manager if you have one, but remember that when productivity drops and the shenanigans start, it will more than likely end up in *your* lap.

Three Hour-itis

I would like to throw a medical or psychological theory out here. I have no medical schooling or education; however, as a father to five children (four of them girls) I would like to think that I have achieved some form of credibility or pseudo degree in the study of sociology.

I believe I have discovered a fascinating, yet undocumented syndrome that plagues the retail and service business employee population. I have shared my findings with hundreds of business owners from the fast food, retail shopping and other service industries where employees aged between sixteen and twenty-one are employed. I also believe that this syndrome can hold place with the other crazy syndromes like "Foreign Accent Syndrome" and

"Walking Corpse Syndrome" (all real by the way). I was going to throw "Restless Leg Syndrome" in here as another off the wall condition, but amazingly this one seems to have some cred in the medical world.

My discovery is "Three Hour-itis." It may be commonly mistaken for its close cousin "Four Hour-itis" and has some similar symptoms but you will find that 3HI (as I commonly call it) is much more common and destructive to younger employees.

3HI symptoms include the following:

- Glazed eyeballs and distant staring for prolonged periods
- Diminished ability to acknowledge audible instructions
- Slowed fine motor skills
- Increased desire to discuss extracurricular activities
- Disinterest in assigned tasks and responsibilities

Three Hour-itis can also bring on multiple and repetitive visits to the bathroom while simultaneously checking on texts, tweets and posts.

Amazingly, all of the symptoms occur at the exact same time; you guessed it, three hours into an assigned work shift at your business. Many employers can easily recognize the warning signs and symptoms, and if not treated quickly, 3HI can very quickly spread like an epidemic through the work place.

Thankfully, 3HI can be easily treated by only assigning employees to three or four-hour shifts. Thankfully, this simple and effective treatment has very few side effects and can almost instantly eradicate 3HI from the workplace. I find that when I have a smaller number of employees working longer shifts, 3HI becomes more rampant. However, if I employ more people and work them shorter and staggered shifts, the debilitating effects of 3HI are not present in the store. Take my word for it, you don't want an outbreak of 3HI rearing its ugly head in your place of business.

Chapter 16   Ongoing Training

One of the key points in maintaining a high level of work by employees is to provide ongoing training. There are many companies that provide training online particularly competency-based training where an employee has to pass certain levels in order to either maintain their current job description or to be promoted.

These work well but what has always been reported to me and what has worked well in my retail locations has been a regular sit down meeting with my crew. Usually this happens every six weeks or so. You would like to think that everyone would make it a priority to attend this meeting. However, with different schedules and other activities, it is always a challenge to get the majority if not all the crew there at one particular time.

These meetings are not mandatory but employees should make an effort to attend these meetings regularly. The best times for my retail experience have always been on a Saturday morning around 9 o'clock or so. Unless you are serving some form of breakfast menu this typically seems to work well.

Motivation to Attend
Of course this is a paid meeting and your employees will be paid for the hour or so that you will meet with them, although some employees will respond to a little more incentive from time to time.

I have always tried to do a little non-meeting time by providing breakfast for them. Generally the ten or fifteen minutes it takes for me to flip pancakes will get enough conversation going that some of the best takeaways from these meetings will be from this informal time.

The Agenda

You should have a set agenda and a set start and finish time. Your attendance will rapidly decline meeting after meeting if you waffle on (pardon the pun) for over an hour about topics that these kids really aren't interested in on a Saturday morning. Keep the meeting precise, fluid and on time.

Your agenda should look something like this.

Reviewing the Agenda and notes from last meeting

Follow up is key in our business. If employees repeatedly report issues to you or other management, or make recommendations that are never followed up on or implemented, you lose credibility with the most important asset you have in business—your employees.

Taking some time to cover progress (or lack thereof) of previously raised items gives employees validation to continue to make recommendations and suggestions to improve your business.

Previous incidents or events to be discussed

Each business should have some form of diary or a hub for employees to record incidents that happen on a daily basis. These incidents may be as miniscule as reporting that a customer wanted a refund because she felt the quality of your product wasn't as it should be.

It should also include events such as employees or customers being injured in some way or any other disturbance or noteworthy event.

These should be covered and any appropriate action taken in order to ensure that the event does not happen again or can at least to be avoided by some way, shape or form.

Business training

I am a big believer in educating your employees as to the financial health of your business. I am not talking about revealing your net profit or how much money you made last year but more so on the principles that make your business successful. I think you would be surprised at the lack of knowledge that most younger employees have on how the business they work in actually makes their money. I'm talking about net profit not gross revenue.

I know from personal experience that employees who are counting the till at the end of the day will comment to each other about the fact that Mr. C didn't even come into the store today and he made $1400. Obviously I didn't make $1400 out of that revenue. Depending what bills are due I might not make anything at all however most younger employees have no idea about the financial commitments you have to your vendors, your landlord and other partners that you utilize in the running of your business.

Spending time on the cost of goods and labor percentages is very important. Your employees should have a solid understanding as to why you have a waste or discount policy, why you send people home when it's raining or overlap shifts in order to reduce labor cost. Educating your employees as to the intricate details of how your business remains successful not only teaches them the process of business management, which in turn leads to educating the younger community, but it also teaches them to care about the principles in your business.

New products or procedures

Every retail business should change up their menu or offerings semi-regularly. The frequent use of limited time offers, or LTOs, in the national and international food chains should give you an idea as to how successful these programs can be. Having a plan to develop LTO menu items and introduce them to your menu should be a part of this meeting. Some of the best suggestions I have ever received so far as menu development have come from our employees. Let me also say that some of the most ridiculous suggestions also came from the same employees.

That being said, when the creative juices start flowing, make sure you have someone write this information down as one Golden Nugget of thought that could revolutionize your menu and also bring in new streams of revenue.

Portion control

In our line of business, portion control is king. Regularly over scooping or even under scooping can not only have a financial impact on the business but can also upset customers. A gentleman who came into one of our Australian locations commented after receiving his cone from me that he had been in the store the night before and got almost double the ice cream for the same amount of money.

Utilizing a scale that can be adjusted to record multiple decimal points and having a scooping or portioning competition not only teaches very important principles but can also make the meeting more enjoyable for the participants.

Health issues

Hopefully you won't have to spend too much time every meeting correcting infractions of the health department regulations. This is basic information that should be covered in the initial training portion of their employment.

You will find these days that health department inspections and the infractions can be almost a part of daily news. Years ago we simply shrugged off employees touching our food. Nowadays with social and digital media pumping out news from all over the country we are hearing more and more about food poisoning and foodborne illnesses. A quick overview of principles like hand washing and glove policies certainly do not go astray. Companies such as Brevis create teaching tools, posters and awards for areas such as hand washing and personal cleanliness. Go to www.hopelesstohero.com for more information

General information and feedback

This is your opportunity to turn the time over to your employees for their thoughts, suggestions and grievances. Many business owners dread this portion of the meeting. However, the more opportunity they have to speak as a group or individually, the less some of these situations build up and gain momentum. In one of these open forum sessions, one of our employees asked about an employee of the month program.

At first I thought it was just another way for this bunch of kids to withdraw more out of my financial and emotional bank account. We set some ground rules and also set some expectations as to how the program would work. You might not use an employee of the month program but may institute a similar type of employee motivation. I will touch on this more in the employee motivation section however the results were very, very surprising to me. Having set all of the ground rules to the program in our employee meeting, the program ran very successfully and increased our employees' work performance and their attitude towards the success of the business.

Utilizing these agenda items and including some of your own not only maintains positive contact with your crew but also gives them a voice and validation within your business. This ongoing training program, which re-enforces your initial training, can be an invaluable asset to the growth of your business and the relationship you have with your employees.

One more point on employee feedback. Some situations warrant the ability for employees to give feedback anonymously—either events are occurring in the workplace that a conscious-driven employee wants to advise you of, or the simple fact that some employees wish to be anonymous when conveying information. Having a way for employees to get notes or information to you can create a valuable stream of information. It could be a simple as some employees slacking off or bringing laptops to work to complete college assignments, or more serious information on theft or harassment in the work place.

As we have always had a safe in our storeroom with most of our businesses, I have encouraged employees to drop a note in the safe of which only I have the combination. (It also helps to be a handwriting expert.) You will find an example of our training agenda at www.hopelesstohero.com.

Chapter 17   Emotional Ownership

The best way to get the most out of your employees and keep them motivated is to give them ownership in your business. I think we all agree that no one is committed to the business like you, the owner. One of the most frustrating principles in dealing with employees is they just don't get it like you do. This is made plainly obvious in the results of the survey mentioned in the introduction.

"I want them to care about the business."

Of course their motivations are very different. You are motivated financially. You have a financial investment in the growth and survival of your business. You want to satisfy customers to not only return and give you repeat business but also to tell their friends and relatives. You want your customers to have the best possible experience in your business.

You also have a time and effort investment. Many business owners in the retail and service industry dedicate many more hours to the success of their business than they get paid for. This time invested may not reap financial rewards immediately, but it will eventually add to the success of your business.

Your employees simply do not have that same motivation, the same investment. The fact of the matter is that many teen employees today do not *need* a job. Standard of living in the western world has changed substantially since you, I and in particular, our parents had to work in the school years. The motivation in the youth of today is simply to get away from home for a couple of hours a day or for some extra spending money. For some it's simply to get through to the end of the shift. They have no real care about the growth of your business or perhaps the satisfaction of your customers as you do. This is the key issue in employee motivation. When you come to understand the basic human principle that nobody puts any more effort into a project than they are going to get back, you are halfway there. It's all about return on investment. With little invested, there is little returned.

One very effective way to give them that deeper understanding and care of the business is to give them ownership. I'm not talking about physical or financial ownership but more so emotional ownership. If they owned some of your business, then their attitudes would change and they would start caring about your customers' experience and the quality of your products.

Think of the youth that starts his or her own lawn mowing business or paper delivery route (when there used to be paper delivery routes). Because these youths had a vested interest in the process of growing the business and keeping customers happy, they were much more engaged in the day-to-day elements of the business. And not only were these youths more conscientious in their own small business, they more than likely went on to own larger businesses. The key in this kind of attitude was ownership—having some skin in the game.

With no investment in your business, your employees show up, do their time with the least amount of effort, and countdown that time, minute by minute until they clock out.

Who Paints a Rented House?

Similar to financial ownership where there is an investment of hard dollars, emotional ownership is where time, effort, reputation and character is invested. This investment comes by way of being attached if not financially but emotionally to the success of your business.

Have you ever taken your rental car through a car wash? Do you see people who are renting a house take the time, effort and money to repaint that house. It rarely happens because again there is no ownership in it. Why should I put my time, money and energy into something that I will reap no benefit from?

Policing studies in many different countries have found a distinct correlation between this level of emotional ownership and crime rates in certain neighborhoods. A study was conducted comparing two areas of a particular town that had a row of vacant buildings. In one area the buildings were overseen and monitored by neighboring residents. They had no physical ownership in the buildings other than an emotional investment in their community. Whenever stray graffiti appeared, they would organize a work detail to scrub it clean. If a window in one of the vacant buildings was smashed they would contact the owner to advise of the situation, and a glazier was summoned to repair the damage.

Compare this scenario to a similar situation across the opposite side of town. This community was in an almost identical situation with their cross-town counterparts, although there was no follow up with any of the damage or vandalism. In fact, this community was suffering from a real "It's not my problem" or "I'm minding my own business" mindset. Within months graffiti grew at an alarming rate, more and more windows and eventually doors were smashed and squatters then moved into the vacant lots. Before long, crime in the community spread from this small row of vacant buildings to most homes in the neighborhood becoming victims of crime.

This is probably the mindset that your current employees have with your business right now. When you really think about it, this is a terrible situation. With no anticipation of a reward or gain, employees will continue to strive for mediocre or the minimum standard to keep their hours and their pay rolling in. They adopt a "mind my own business" attitude which converts to an "it's not my job" mentality.

Responsibility Breeds Respect

So how do you get your employees to be more invested in your business. Well I will tell you that putting people in charge of an activity, event or happening and allowing them to see the results of some organizational and other efforts can really attach them to the success of your business. One of the most successful ways in getting employees to experience emotional ownership in your business is by way of assignment or task giving.

Nothing feels better than putting your energy and efforts into an activity or assignment and seeing that activity through the planning stage. When the execution is complete and the event is over, there is a great deal of satisfaction knowing that you achieved great results through your effort. This feeling can be extremely strong even when there is no monetary reward attached to them.

When employees are given tasks from a monotonous and unchanging list on the wall each and every time they come into the store, they have no sense of pride or accomplishment when the list is completed. You probably don't congratulate or thank them for completing the list either because you feel that this is part of their basic responsibility. "This is what I am paying them for," you mutter to yourself. Thus the uncaring and unmotivated employee cycle continues to roll on and on and on.

Open Days

Let me give you an example. At the grand opening for one of our locations I had many activities that I wanted to conduct on our open day. Some of the activities included face painting, a "name the cow" competition and an ice cream eating competition. There was also a "wheel of ice cream" and a coloring competition where kids could win a bike. I placed each of our shift supervisors in charge of a committee of two or three people to plan and execute each of these activities. I gave them guidelines and a goal that I would like to see achieved at the end of their assignment.

Each committee went headfirst into their assignment by meeting at the store and brainstorming with their committee members about what would be the best way to achieve their goals. Some of these meetings happened in work time however I was amazed that members of the crew would come in during their time off, just to participate in their particular committee meeting. The committee head or the entire committee would also meet with me when needed for approval of expenditure or just to review the plans in general. A week before the event, we all met together and rolled out our plans.

Needless to say that when the big day rolled around, everybody was extremely excited and engaged in their own particular activity. Sure things did not go exactly as I would've planned it. Take for example the cow box that was created for the competition entries.

It looked a little "hokey" to me; however, the way it was presented on the day and the smiles that were on the faces of those committee members taught me that the little inconsistencies were a fair trade for the emotional investment these kids had in the activity.

Despite some bad weather, the day was a complete success. Not just in retail sales but in the investment made by these employees into my business. Many of the kids asked what the next event was going to be or had ideas for a weekly or monthly activity that they would like to organize. All of a sudden coming into work meant more than just processing orders and scooping ice cream.

It became a place of inspiration and brainstorming. I was relatively welcoming of any idea or activity that was proposed not because of the customer engagement or the finance it would bring in, but more to see the reaction and excitement all of our employees. This was a huge motivational tool.

Assign a Specialist

I am going to get a little personal here with a little toilet talk.

A few years ago we broke the china lid to the toilet cistern in our basement. Unfortunately there are no replacement lids available for a twenty-year-old toilet cistern and I was put in a situation where I would either have to search the black market for a Kohler H2260 cistern lid or replace the whole system. I opted for number one (pardon the pun) and put some feelers out in the toilet community for a used lid supplier.

To my astonishment, there is the "guy" called Larry who works out of a non-descript hardware store in St. Louis who is known as "the toilet lid guy." I learned about his existence from a friend of a friend of a friend who wanted to remain anonymous. I attended the store and asked lady at the front counter for Larry. "Someone's here for Larry," she called back to the nether regions of the showroom.

I was escorted to a solid steel black door with a sliding rectangular peephole. It slid open abruptly. "I'm here to see Larry," I said sheepishly. The peephole slid shut, and the steel door creaked open and closed again behind me. After I was patted down, I was led to a smoky room where Larry was seated on an oversized leather toilet seat.

OK so that last bit was a bit of overkill, but the point here is that there actually is a Larry and he actually specializes in toilet lids.

Now in the myriad of tasks that your employees are assigned to do, I am sure that there are a couple of shining stars in each area of responsibility. In my line of business there may be only two girls out of my twenty employees who are really great at rolling waffle cones. Or perhaps you have an employee who outshines the others on the point of sale or register system. Regardless of what task it is, there is an opportunity here to assign a couple of your employees as specialists.

The US Government calls them "Czars." We had two "Waffle Cone Czars" working for us who have overall responsibly to ensure that our waffle cones are always top rated and other employees are up on their skills. The waffle cone czars reported straight to the general manager or owner and could convene their own training sessions and standards. Again, this is an opportunity to keep employees invested in your business. When they feel as though they make a difference or have some extra responsibility, it can make a huge difference as to their work performance and overall attitude.

How is a czar rewarded? It may be a slightly higher pay point, but it could also be as simple as a title on a name badge or the responsibility of being an authority on one particular element of your business. Their importance relates directly to how valuable you make them feel in this role. If you plan to meet with them monthly or give them time in training meetings, this validates their position and responsibility and communicates to them that this is not merely a hollow title they wear.

I cannot stress enough the value that the principle of Emotional Ownership can have in your business. Getting employees to "care" about your business is one of the greatest challenges you will face in the running of your business. Having employees receive a return on their investment in your business will keep them engaged and excited to see the collective business grow.

A Word on Delegation

There is a mentality with entrepreneurs and business owners that no one can do the job as good as they can. That there is a vision in the mind as to how a particular plan, event or process looks and accompanied with that vision is a reluctance to acknowledge that anyone else could execute that plan. There is danger here of becoming so bogged down with the details that the plan or vision is never really executed properly because of the many other plans and visions in your head.

Some of the greatest lessons of business management were taught by William McKnight, CEO of 3M. His business philosophy and management style have been taught in books, seminars and workshops throughout the world. His wisdom on delegation and growing employees through tasks and responsibilities is particularly beneficial.

"If you put fences around people; you get sheep. Give people the room that they need." [1]

"As our business grows, it becomes increasingly necessary to delegate responsibility and to encourage men and women to exercise their initiative. This requires considerable tolerance. Those men and women, to whom we delegate authority and responsibility, if they are good people, are going to want to do their jobs in their own way."

---

[1] William McKnight.

"Mistakes will be made. But if a person is essentially right, the mistakes he or she makes are not as serious in the long run as the mistakes management will make if it undertakes to tell those in authority exactly how they must do their jobs."

"Management that is destructively critical when mistakes are made kills initiative. And it's essential that we have many people with initiative if we are to continue to grow."

As you utilize the principle of delegation in the workplace, you will see emotional ownership grow and the investment that your employees will make in your business multiply.

Chapter 18   Rewards and Motivation

So apart from assignments and other committees that you may have your employees participate in, there other types of motivational activities available to get the most out of your employees on an ongoing basis.

Let's look at the three great motivators. These motivators have been in play within relationships for thousands of years and are the root driving force behind why we do what for someone else. As an employee fulfills his responsibility or duty, he is motivated to do so by three main reasons—fear, duty and love.

Fear

A business scenario where an employee is motivated by fear is not a good one. Sure the work may be getting done but the action is only accomplished through a negative drive or fear of a negative consequence.

This fear may come as a result of you as the employer frequently erupting and yelling at your employees. There may also be a "perceived" fear of this occurring where this behavior may not have been witnessed, but the employee feels that you are close to a breaking point by your expressions or body language. This fear may also come as a result of the fear of losing their job or other financial consequence.

Motivation by way of fear does not create loyal and hard-working employees. It does not encourage crewmembers to go above and beyond the call of duty. Rather the opposite happens. Employees will only attain the minimum standard or mediocre work performance to placate the boss. All they have to do is reach the standard that pacifies the owner or employer so that stamping of feet and "spitting of the dummy" does not occur.

Duty

An employee who is motivated by duty is not a bad employee. In fact this is an employee with a clear and driven conscience. Perhaps the principle of duty was taught to them by their parents or other persons of authority like teachers or scoutmasters. The principle of accomplishing tasks motivated by duty is a valued character trait that runs through the core of traditional family values, respect and honor for those in authority.

Motivation by a sense of duty is more valuable than being motivated by fear, but still does not transcend going above and beyond the minimum standard of work performance.

Love

Being motivated by love does not connote any romantic or "lovey dovey" scenarios. This love we speak of is more the honor, respect, charity and overall "caring" for the business and for those who work in it. Having employees motivated by their love of coming to work, or meeting with your customers is the highest level of motivation.

We have heard it said hundreds of times. If you love your job, you will never have to "work" a day in your life. The term "work" here denotes drudgery and disdain for the workplace—the kind of work an employee does when he is motivated by fear or duty alone. As mentioned in the previous chapter, giving employees passion and love of work can be easily achieved and highly rewarding for all parties.

So what types of rewards and motivations work the best?

Competency Based Payroll

Having some framework of initial training or a competency based probation system is always a good way to start an employee off in your business. This kind of program identifies key competencies in which your employees should be competent with. This program can be multi-level but there certainly should be a minimum standard that has to be achieved before the new hire achieves some form of increased pay.

Let me give you an example. When a new employee started in our business, they started on minimum wage. The minimum wage at that time was $7.25 an hour. The entire front counter workers, no matter who they were or from where they were sourced, started at this level. These employees were teamed with a shift manager, designated trainer or czar to teach them the core competencies that we required of all our employees before they moved up the scale in pay.

In our business, which was focused on ice cream and frozen desserts, they had to achieve competency in the following elements:

- ✓ Customer greeting,
- ✓ POS or register system,
- ✓ Portion control techniques,
- ✓ Product making ability,
- ✓ Cash handling requirements
- ✓ Waffle cone making
- ✓ Shift supervisory duties and so forth.

You may obviously have different focal areas and responsibilities when it comes to your particular business; however, it is important to draft up a list of competencies that you require your employees to achieve as a minimum standard of work in your business. Sure, not everyone is going to be a star at customer service or be able to make the perfect waffle cone. But you need to come up with the minimum standard of performance and ensure that each employee can meet the minimum standard in order for you to have success with your employees. Not only does this raise the general standard of performance for your employees but it also gives them motivation, as an increase in pay, albeit $.25 an hour, is still motivation enough to want to achieve a higher level of performance.

You should also have the system in place for your management or assistant managers who are looking for opportunities to earn more money to receive more responsibility.

Employee Rewards

As previously mentioned, one of our girls brought up the idea of an employee of the month program, and at first I shuddered.

First of all, how do you determine who is worthy of being employee of the month, and secondly, who will defend the choice of the person (and the person themselves) when the uprising occurs on the day of the big announcement. Surely all of the employees will think they are worthy of the accolade in some way, shape or form. This being said, I agreed that it would be a good way to motivate our people, so we instituted it. I must say, I have been surprised as to what has ensued as a result of that announcement.

Our employees have shown great aptitude and frankly, moments of brilliance. Let me give you an example. We had an annual St. Patrick's Day promotion with the local Girl Guides Group where we bought bulk boxes of cookies from them and advertised a "Thin Mint Concrete" (where we mixed our custard up in a blender with the Girl Guides Thin Mint cookies). I wanted to advertise this item on our monument sign outside our shop. However, we only had a certain number of letters for the board, and we soon ran out of T's. I asked Jon, one of our employees, to do his best to make both sides of the board read the same, despite the shortage of letters.

I drove past the shop later that evening and noticed that both sides of our monument board read the same (just as I had asked Jon to do) but knowing that we had a shortage of T's, I was puzzled as to how this came about. Upon closer inspection, Jon had inverted two of the letter L's and overlapped them to create extra T's. I was both amazed and excited at the same time. Not because we would sell more Thin Mint concretes, but at Jon's ingenuity and creative thinking. Now that's "Employee of the Month" material. It may seem to the average reader to be a simple act, but think for a moment if Jon's work ethic had been just to attain "minimum standard." He could have easily justified only completing one side of the board, but because he had been empowered to care about the business and the role he played there, he rose above that standard that was asked of him.

I also challenged the crew to eclipse our sales numbers from the previous owner's monthly sales from last season. First month's reward was taking them all to the movies. Second month, I would treat them all to a laser tag night. Both of these rewards would end up only costing me one or two hundred dollars, but the incentive to be bigger and better this year seemed to really stick with the crew. The reward is relatively small in the grand scheme of things however, any recognition, large or small, is always a positive and helps build camaraderie and our team spirit.

These sales based rewards may also come in the form of payroll bonuses, employee parties, and any other events that seem appropriate.

Motivation and Upselling

There are a slew of motivational games and activities that are relatively easy to organize and can help employees feel more engaged and increase sales at the same time.

Sometimes these activities are driven simply by breaking up the monotony of the workday or can have some kind of financial benefit for your employees. They may include a "best dressed" or costume competition for a particular celebration of year such as Ugly Christmas sweaters or Halloween costumes.

Here are a couple of examples.

The Word Game

Give your server a specific word that they have to use in their welcome pitch without having the customer comment on it. For example you may have a container with the word strips therein and each server needs to pick a word before she serves the customer. Words like Alligator, Chainsaw, Umbilical and Prism may be words in the hat. If Alex can give his "welcome" pitch and use the word "Umbilical" without being questioned or called out by the customer, he gets a point. Most points at the end of the shift wins.

The $20 Game

On a selected day the business owner might make an announcement that today is the $20 game day. You can't do this game all the time as it loses its sparkle, but when played selectively, it can be a great motivator for your employees to upsell and to engage with customers a little better.

A clean crisp $20 bill is taken from your wallet and held above your head. Then an announcement is made that today is the $20 game day. The premise of the game is simple. Whoever gets the highest sales of the day wins the $20.

This game motivates the employees to engage a little more with the customer and to go through the process of upselling to try and increase the sale they are making. This game necessitates that multiple people have access to the register so each can take turns in serving customers.

Let's say Susie serves the first customer of the day, a little old lady who generally does not spend anything more than the kiddie cone. When grandma checks out the first sale of the day is registered at $3.77. By virtue of the first sale of the day Susie now is the front runner in the $20 game.

Julie is also working with Susie and gets to serve the next customer a portly man who works at the car dealership down the road. He comes in three times a week for his double scoop sundae and when he hands over the cash of $7.22, Julie now takes the lead in the $20 game.

Alex serves the next customer and their potential order comes to $6.90 so Alex starts the process of upselling. He politely asks the customer if they would like a pint or a quart to take home with them. The employee with the highest sales of the day wins the $20.

Pick an Upsell Item

You may play a similar game that focuses on one particular product or service that you offer. Let's say that our pint freezer is looking relatively full and we need some motivated sales people to move the inventory so that we can reload and refresh our products.

He (or she) who sells the most pints this weekend receives a $20 gift card. Again, a small investment can return great profits with the right focus.

It seems like all fun and games, but let me advise you on two areas of concern with some of these activities. The first of which is to ensure that there is equal opportunity for all to be involved. Opening up competitions and prizes to just the servers and leaving out the back of the house support crew can drive a deep chasm between both groups. Perhaps rotate certain crews working for certain shifts and have your efforts concentrate on winning as a team. This will build team spirit and support among your employees.

Secondly, let's not lose focus of our core goal to have the customer feel appreciated and welcomed. Obviously these games are meant to make the workplace interesting and challenging but cannot be at the expense of customers feeling harassed or railroaded into purchasing decisions.

With the right focus and a little oversight, these motivations and rewards can be a fun and effective way of increasing revenue and employee engagement.

A Simple Thank You

You would be probably be surprised to discover that one of the greatest motivators in the workplace is being appreciated and acknowledged by your employer by knowing you have made a significant contribution to the business or a common cause.

The church I attend is a volunteer based church—a lay clergy. This means that the administration and operation of each church unit, parish or ward, is run by members of the congregation who are assigned different roles and responsibilities. One year you could be asked to be the hymn book collector, and the next you could be the scout leader for the youth. Assignments and responsibilities run the gamut of teaching young children in Sunday school to serving as the parish leader, or bishop, of the ward.

Obviously these responsibilities have differing levels of time, commitment and stress. I found myself serving as the bishop of our ward, the parish leader if you will, for a period of about four years. At one particular time during this period, we had three ice cream locations, a young family and were building our dream home—ourselves. It was certainly a period of time when resource management and planning with each role sometimes pulled in different directions.

Being bishop of the ward required a great commitment of time and focus, not only for me, but also for my wife and family who often went without husband/father time while a greater need was being fulfilled. I recall one Tuesday evening while I was at the office at our church. I had just finished giving a young couple counsel on a matter that was very emotional and important to them, and I felt very drained. I had the distinct feeling that I was trying to fill too many roles at one time and felt that I wasn't really accomplishing anything in any of them—just running in the hamster wheel. While I was thus contemplating my inadequacy, I saw a note slip under the office door.

By the time I had gotten up and opened the door, the deliverer had vanished—obviously a clandestine operation. I sat back down at my desk and opened the envelope. Inside was a simple anonymous handwritten note.

> *Dear Bishop Christensen.*
> *This is just a quick note to say*
> *that we appreciate all that you*

do. Your quiet efforts do not go
unnoticed. Thanks.

Now I don't relay this communication to self-aggrandize or imply I worked harder than anyone else in the area, but I will tell you that this little note, a simple as it was, made an enormous difference to my whole view of life as I knew it back then. I have many times since remembered that small charitable act of appreciation and encouragement. I don't think the author could really comprehend the difference those few words made in my life at that time. It didn't take money or a gift wrapped little widget to communicate the appreciation—just a couple of simple, heart felt words. "Thank you." I think they are words we don't say or hear enough.

Apple Pear Juice

Everyone loves to hear what a good job they have done. A student relishes a report card that shows a high achievement as their scholastic achievement. It is a real shot in the arm and has a "motivatory" effect to continue studying hard.

As an employee, are we pleased when a previous customer has reported to our manager or employer what an outstanding job we did for them? While participating in the retail experience as a customer, I often make comment to a shift supervisor or manager that I would like to nominate a helpful staff member as the "Employee of the Month." Now granted a lot of businesses don't have or run that program, but it is a quick and effective verbal form of rewarding good customer service.

As a business owner, I am grateful to hear back from my customers, that my staff members "are the best around" or "treat my family like kings." "You have a great bunch of kids working here" is music to my ears. So let's keep the music playing. How often have you commented on a good experience you had in someone's store, on that flight, or in that restaurant?

Years ago, when my wife and I were out shopping, a particular type of juice caught my eye and I thought I'd run it up the flagpole and see how it tasted. I still remember the brand very vividly, it was Just Juice and the flavor was "Apple/Pear." When we got home and tasted the juice for the first time, I was amazed. It was the most delicious juice I had tasted in years. I said to my wife, "I'm going to call these guys up and tell them what a great job they have done with this juice." I dialed the 800 number off the box (which I assume no one ever calls) and was immediately put through to the operator.

"My name is Steve Christensen, and I have just bought a container or your Apple/Pear at the grocery store, and I want to talk to someone about it."

"Oh!" exclaimed the operator, "let me see who I can get for you." She sounded concerned. The phone rang a couple more times and another lady answered, "Customer service?"

"My name is Steve Christensen, and I have just bought a container or your Apple/Pear at the grocery store, and I want to talk to someone about it."

"Oh um, would you like someone in administration or production?"

"Production, please."

"I'll put you through."

"Hello production, this is Gerry."

"Hi, Gerry, my name is Steve Christensen, and I have just bought a container or your Apple/Pear at the grocery store, can I talk to you about it?"

"Oh um, I'll...just put you on to the production manager."

I was put on hold for a couple of minutes, while, no doubt, the production manager was briefed on the incoming call.

"Hello, this is Mike, how can I help you?" There was tension in his voice.

"Hi, Mike, my name is Steve Christensen, and I have just bought a container or your Apple/Pear at the grocery store, and I want to talk to you about it."

The air was very tense and I could sense he feared the worst. "Ah... yes, you can talk to me."

"Mike, this Apple/Pear juice is the best juice I have tasted in all my life, and I just wanted to call up and congratulate you on it. A job well done!"

There was silence on the line. "Are you there, Mike?"

"Oh yeah, well thanks!" Mike breathes a sigh of relief. "Actually," he said, "it's good to hear that because we brought it out a while ago and..." blah, blah, blah. I couldn't shut him up for about five minutes.

Why is it we only call when we are disappointed, outraged or let down? Everyone I spoke to in the organization was ready for the worst. We as a society need to turn that around and start taking the time to reward the good work done that many take for granted, particularly if we are not dealing directly with the person who needs to hear the feedback.

The Gift of Thanks

There are many different ways you convey your appreciation to your employees. Please don't think that a heartfelt thank you to the crew, either individually or collectively, isn't enough. When an employee is taken aside and told that they really do great work, and you very much appreciate their attitude and work ethic, this has an amazing effect on the psyche. The publication, *Psychology Today* stated that saying "thank you" is mostly an emotional act. It connects one person to another. Saying "thank you" doesn't just acknowledge someone's effort, thoughtfulness, intent, or action. It acknowledges the person himself."

It is a simple act that doesn't take a lot of time, and effort, but it does take thought. Perhaps right now take some time to go over the list of employees in your mind and I am sure a couple of names will jump out as your stellar employees. Make a mental or physical note to let them know that you appreciate the way they do their business.

Chapter 19 Building a Business Culture

Recently our family was invited to a dance recital of cultural significance. Friends of our family had prepared a special event to celebrate the achievements of one of their daughters, Trishna, in the field of Bharatanatyam, which being interpreted means "Indian dance."

The program included special comments and congratulations from family, friends and Trishna's dance instructor; however, the feature of the evening was watching Trishna perform numerous dance routines she had painstakingly learned through years of practice and study. Her talent illustrated her magnificent ability to relate legends and stories through music and movement, and her years of hard work and dedication to the art were very evident.

Combine the brilliance of period costumes and the stirrings of traditional music, and we were left with an event that culturally enriched our family. We felt privileged to be invited and we shared our gratitude with our hosts.

Our family also shared another cultural event with this family, which also left an impression. We were invited to a traditional Indian meal at their home. A personal favorite my mine from the sub-continent is Lamb Korma and although not a fan of hugely spiced food, this dish, when prepared correctly delicately balances sharp spices and sweet coconut cream. We were placed at the dinner table in such a manner that I was seated next to granny who resides in India but visits every summer.

To my surprise I observed that while the rest of us dined on expertly prepared Indian cuisine, granny was tucking into a bowl of mac and cheese. I tried to hold my peace but couldn't resist asking why granny was feverishly consuming the Kraft. Again, I was taught a lesson on culture. When granny visits the USA, she eats the food of the USA. I know many of you reading this will be shocked that some (if not many) foreigners consider mac and cheese to be a culinary tradition of this country, but in granny's perception it was.

Could it be true that a periodic change in culture can be as refreshing and enjoyable as traditions accepted for a considerable period of time?

Culture Is Something to be Fostered and Nurtured.

Whether it is in the realm of traditional dance or in the workplace, a positive culture and can inspire, motivate and in some cases, lift individuals to greater heights. There is much to be said about fostering a tradition of positive culture among employees in the workplace and the effect that it has on employees and customers alike. Tony Hsieh (pronounced Shay), has a fascinating business history and an equally engaging view on how culture affects businesses, both big and small. Speaking regularly on the motivational and business seminar circuit, his statements like the following invoke and inspire managers and employers to high culture levels.

"Businesses often forget about the culture, and ultimately, they suffer for it because you can't deliver good service from unhappy employees."

Hsieh, the CEO of Zappos, the online shoe (and everything else) store, has made a career and a lot of money from focusing on his company's culture. Upon selling his startup company "Link Exchange" to Microsoft for 265 million dollars, he set about to turn Zappos' failing market share in the online footwear category.

Hsieh states, "At Zappos, our belief is that if you get the culture right, most of the other stuff — like great customer service, or building a great long-term brand, or passionate employees and customers — will happen naturally on its own."

"Your culture is your brand. So how do you build and maintain the culture that you want? It starts with the hiring process."

In fact, Zappos employees have broken their culture down to ten effective core values that employees at any level of the company are encouraged to embrace.

1. Deliver WOW through Service
2. Embrace and Drive Change
3. Create Fun and a Little Weirdness

4. Be Adventurous, Creative, and Open-Minded
5. Pursue Growth and Learning
6. Build Open and Honest relationships with Communication
7. Build a Positive Team and Family Spirit
8. Do More with Less
9. Be Passionate and Determined
10. Be Humble

Looking at the past history and performance of Hsieh's company ownership, I think every small business owner could take a page out of his book—that book being *Delivering Happiness*. You can find it at your local good book store or of course at www.zappos.com. There are many great lessons to be learned from a culture warrior who paved the way before us. When you research the best companies to work for within an industry or a particular country, you will find the one principle that the entire top ten businesses have in common is the focus on building a positive culture in the workplace.

Take for instance Google. Google has always ranked in the top ten companies to work for, and for good reason. The perks of working for the largest gatherer of information on the planet are unmatched. The corporate complex is dotted with bocce courts, a bowling alley and the benefits just keep stacking up. In the New York office, employees can have their eyebrows shaped for free. And no one beats the culinary benefits. One Google employee reports that workers are never more than 150 feet away from a well-stocked pantry.

These are lessons that can be scaled down and applied to any business, shop or retail outlet to enrich to workplace and get a more positive experience from your crew. Before you start laying the laminate wood down for your personal bowling alley, let me give you some brief and simpler examples:

Ring My Bell

I can't say for sure whether all of their locations practice this same principle, however I was visiting an A&W Root beer stand a couple of years ago in a business capacity. I could not help but notice every couple of minutes that a distant bell would ring and all of the employees would yell out "hey" or "yeah" in unison. It got to the point where I was twenty minutes into my business there, and had to stop and ask the shop owner what all the jocularity was about. He took me to a sign posted on the doorframe below a small bell. The sign was easily visible to customers leaving, although I had missed it on the way in. The sign simply read,

"Please ring the bell if you have had a great experience in our store today."

In response to the sound of the bell, all of the employees in earshot would respond with shouts of joy and gratitude. It was a very simple idea, and easily executed, yet the resulting interaction between customer and employee left both parties feeling uplifted and appreciated. Pavlov's dog would have been proud and it is something that remained with me for many years.

When customers and employees feel valued and appreciated, the shop environment and the subsequent sales are elevated. As mentioned in the previous chapter once we started setting sales goals for our crew the culture of being rewarded for the crew's efforts was definitely appreciated. It's not the amount of money involved here. It's the collaboration of a team effort that not only amounted to hitting a sales goal, but the camaraderie that occurs throughout the process and enjoying the spoils of victory. And sure, I admit it's not a gourmet pantry in the back of the shop, or a grass court in the spirit of Wimbledon, but it's a start.

The Culture of Caring

One more point on your business culture. In order to get your employees to care about what they are doing in the workplace, it is important that they see YOU caring. And not just about the bottom line or whether they are showing up for work on time.

I'm talking about you caring about them. I have touched on the principle of "Being Friendly but not Being their Friend" This is a tough tightrope to balance on. Let me share with you two examples of business owners who really understand, execute and benefit from this Culture of Caring.

Big Pizza – Melbourne, Australia

I recently visited a pizza store in Melbourne, Australia called Big Pizza. Their core menu was...well, big pizzas. They also offered garlic bread, salads and coffee—and not just any coffee, good coffee.

Big Pizza is in a food court on the ground level of a central business district office building. There are about eight to ten other businesses of different description in the food court including a National Coffee chain store, directly opposite the Big Pizza location. It was about 9:30 in the morning when I witnessed what could be called an anomaly in the morning coffee business. Big Pizza had literally thirty to forty people waiting in a line to get coffee there. The specialty coffee location across the hall was vacant—not one soul at the counter. In fact, sometimes the line at Big Pizza gets so long that it ends very close to the door of the coffee concept. Customers happily waited in line for coffee chatting with one another to pass the time.

Why was this happening? I was amazed as I sat and watched the line continue for twenty to thirty minutes. The key element was an owner who acknowledged the importance of his customer service, crew and his customers. David Hachem opened the Big Pizza location about a year ago. Recently on his business' first birthday, he gave away bottles of wine. It is not unusual for David and his crew to give away free muffins with their coffee.

I took some time to talk to Dave to learn about what makes his business so successful. What keeps people lining up and waiting for coffee when they can simply turn on a heel and walk ten steps to another coffee business—one that is nationally franchised?

"It's simple," Dave says. *"Without them I am nothing."*

Dave has a great passion for his business and in particular, his employees; and they in turn pay his enthusiasm forward to their customers. *"You have to thank them. You have to create a happy work environment. It's contagious. New employees can't help but buy into the enthusiastic environment."*

Dave Hachem of Big Pizza, Melbourne, Australia

Dave strives to meet with his team regularly, sometimes weekly, asking them how he and they can improve the business, change things up and satisfy their customers.

"We give to get" is Dave's motto both with his employees and his customers. Dave offers his employees sales goal objectives with monetary rewards for achieving them. His sales goals are incremental with higher weekly sales resulting in greater bonuses for his crew. His employees are extremely engaging and friendly. They know most of their customers by name and what they regularly order. They have to really. There are no menu boards. Sure, there is an indication of size and price, however all of the menu choices for food and beverage are either the food itself on display or they are explained to customers by the crew.

Customers don't miss out on the giving as well. Dave treats everybody as an important part of his business *"Even if they just* *spend $3."* Dave gave free muffins out at Christmas time. *"Giving is so important." "Our customers work in offices here. We like to give them an avenue of relief; a break,"* he says.

At the time of writing Big Pizza did not have a Facebook page, twitter accounts or loyalty cards, although his customers are extremely loyal. His loyalty card is presented in an attitude of appreciation and engagement, and it works. His sales are testament to that. David Hachem and his employees are the poster children for what focusing on hiring, training and motivating can bring—super employees, loyal customers and a successful business.

Four Seas Ice Cream – Cape Cod, New England
One of the doyens of the ice cream industry was Dick Warren. Dick was a very special man, not only to his employees, but to the industry. To tell you the truth, there are not enough pages in this or most other books to tell the life story of a man who really cared about his employees. Dick was the epitome of the word "caring."

Dick was tragically killed in a skiing accident January, 2008 at the ripe old age of seventy-two years. His love of the ice cream business, skiing, the community and his employees is legend around those parts. Dick and his son Doug of Four Seas Ice Cream at Cape Cod were so entrenched in the culture of caring that you could mistake them for family—and they often were.

Often high school and college-aged employees would be playing sports at the highest level and would be asked by teammates if the raucous supporters on the sidelines were their family members. "No, that's my boss," would be the reply.

The "Chief" Dick Warren

Whether it was football, basketball, hockey or other activities, the Warrens would strive to support their employees out-of-work endeavors is if they were their own children. Newspaper articles on employees would also be meticulously cut out and stuck on the stores walls.

It would not be uncommon for Dick and his family to plan their vacations and trips around visiting employees who had moved on or were attending college. Dick would always find the time to take them out to lunch or dinner while he was there. The Warrens held "out of hours" events to also build camaraderie and team spirit between the employees and themselves. Pool parties and meals were common, however the big event was the annual ski trip where the Warrens would (and still do) take their employees on a skiing weekend—all expenses paid.

This ongoing cycle of caring ensured that employees were motivated by the love of the job and the support of their employers. This also resulted in increased work ethic and employees who really cared about the business, their employers and their customers. The Warrens can certainly testify to the return on their investment of time, money and effort they put into this culture of caring. Every year at the close of the ice cream season, it's all hands on deck as current and even alumni employees suit up and prepare for the end of season sell out. For the last ten days or so, Four Seas Ice Cream sells approximately eleven thousand quarts of ice cream to those passionate and loyal customers who are stocking up for a cold winter season.

Super Employees equal Super Growth.

Create Your Own Culture

May I suggest that you put some serious time and thought into the process of your business or work culture. This is a principle that is often overlooked in many small businesses but an essential element in having employees respond and care. One easy way is to make a list of the types of workplaces that you either would like to work in or perhaps some that you have already worked in.

You can also take a page out of some retail or service businesses you have visited as a customer.

- What parts of the job did you like?
- What aspects of a work environment would you like to work in?
- What makes one business that you patronize so much more successful than another?
- Why do you take your business there?

Here is a list of attributes of a positive business culture that may start you off:

Whine Free Zone: Encourage uplifting and encouraging conversation between customers and your fellow employees.

Keep Gossip Free: The only thing worse than talking about someone behind their back is finding out that others are talking about you behind your back. Remember what Grandma Christensen always used to say—if you can't say something nice about someone, don't say anything at all.

Incentivize: Everybody loves to be rewarded for a job well done, so creating incentives for a team that excels will spur them on to greater heights.

Attitude of Gratitude: This is not only good customer service policy but also good employer/employee policy.

Giving Is Better Than Receiving: creating opportunities to serve others or assist local charities gives the team a higher purpose and a gratitude for what they have in their lives.

The Customer Is the Key: As Henry Ford famously said, "The employee only handles the money; it's the customer that pays the wages." Having a customer centric culture results in better business.

Mistakes are OK – As long as we are learning: Learning from mistakes is a valuable part of the learning process. Oscar Wilde stated, "Experience is simply the name we give mistakes."

Chapter 20   In Closing

I do a lot of coaching and seminar leading in the world of frozen desserts. I generally cover every topic including menu development, employee training, marketing and promotion and a plethora of other related topics. Do you know that when question and answer time comes up, the first question is always very similar to the following:

"What is new in the industry?"

To tell you the truth, there is rarely ever any concept or principle that is really "new" within our industry or anyone else's for that matter. What is "new" is the *reformulation* of an existing idea or concept.

The Fizz Cup

I met David Chodosh at a tradeshow in Columbus, Ohio. Dave is a toy designer and worked for many years at Mattel and other well-known toy companies. I noticed Dave working in a booth at the show because there was a line of people numbering fifty plus at his booth waiting to get their hands on his new invention—The Fizz Cup.

The story goes that Dave was with his family at an ice cream store when he witnessed the cardinal sin of root beer float creation—ice cream first and soda second. What resulted was an eruption rivaling Vesuvius. Cogs started turning in Dave's head as they did most times when he witnessed some of life's frustrations and potential fun and interesting inventions to solve them. This is how the Fizz Cup was born. Dave designed a cup that was able to be screwed onto a soda bottle. Ice cream or soft serve would be placed in the top of the removable lid and when the cup was screwed back onto the bottle you could regulate how much of the soda accessed the ice cream by tipping the bottle on the side. Now you have a constantly refreshing, single-handed root beer float on the go.

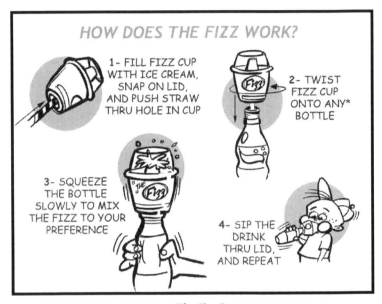

The Fizz Cup

It was certainly a hot item at that show. As soon as someone was seen walking down an aisle sipping on a fizz cup, they were immediately asked where they got it and the rest was tradeshow history. In Dave's mind, it was simply a new "twist" on an old idea. For more of Dave's "eye rolling" puns, watch the fizz video at www.hopelesstohero.com/video.

Similarly, the principles, ideas and concepts in this book are not new. In fact there have probably been a thousand or more books written on this or similar subjects. The challenges and pitfalls of human resources have been around since Noah built the Ark.

Our goal here was to refashion, refresh and remind.

Many of us who own or operate small businesses utilizing employees, already know this information. We have seen these principles work in other business scenarios, but to have a new look at traditional information in a new light seems to motivate us to achieve what every employer or business owner really wants:

To find, train and motivate super employees.

What we are discussing here is not groundbreaking information or some new psychological view of the typical employer/employee relationship. They are core principles that when applied effectively can make a significant difference in your employees' attitudes and motivations in the workplace—in the way they interact with their employer, their fellow workmates and their customers. I would like to think that not only can this have a positive effect on your bottom line, but it can also make the world a little better in your place of business.

Only a Small Percentage Win

If you do some research on the "get rich quick" seminar segment you will find that only a very small percentage of attendees at these events actually follow through and do what they paid thousands of dollars to learn.

For example, there are many seminars available to learn how to flip property or to benefit from foreclosures. For a nominal fee people attend these seminars to learn the elements of becoming wealthy through property management. The fact of the matter is only a small percentage actually follow through after the excitement and energy

201

of the seminar. I have witnessed the same phenomena in my workshops and classes. The excitement and buzz of learning something new and the opportunity to make money at doing it is very intense at the time of the event and shortly thereafter. Unfortunately many people drop off the radar when they settle back into life's regular activities.

Definition of Character

Hyrum Smith, author of the bestselling *The Power of Perception*, penned a very inspirational definition of the term "character."

"Character, simply stated, is doing what you say you are going to do. A more formal definition is: Character is the ability to carry out a worthy decision after the emotion of making that decision has passed."

Please take a moment to read and reread that passage. It is very powerful. If only each of us could follow through and actually accomplish what we get excited about at the moment of commitment. Having character means we no longer let our New Year's Resolution to drop twenty pounds fade into obscurity at the sight of an all you can eat buffet.

Character means the excitement you feel at the beginning of a semester of study and the recommitment you promise to yourself that doesn't fade off after the first big party or "weekend away" invitations. Character also means that when you read a book that inspires you to *do* a little better, or *be* a little better in your business or your life in general, that desire to do better resonates and drives you. My sincere goal is that you put into practice these principles that I know can change your business, your employees and your life.

One Final Thought

Our retail location in St. Louis was our first store in the United States. Our family moved to the US in 2004 not knowing whether we would stay for a couple of years or perhaps for the rest of our lives. We learned to love and appreciate the freedom and opportunity the U.S. offered our family and every other citizen living here. Certainly the small business support mechanism and mentality is much stronger here than in any other country. It truly can be the American dream for everybody to start and grow their own business in whatever realm they want.

I tried to instill this appreciation of opportunity and success into my young employees.

Through some of the principles we have discussed in this book, I would like to think that each of my employees appreciated the opportunity to work, learn and grow in our retail stores. Whenever I left the store to finish a shift, I would always turn to my employees and with outstretched arms, say the following words.

"Guys — My American dream is now in your hands. Please be careful with it. Please don't crush my American dream."

The boys looked at me as if it was just another of Mr. C's crazy rants, but the girls got it. Each individual employee must feel empowered and appreciate the role they can play in the success of your business.

These employees, both yours and mine, have the potential to grow or diminish our businesses. Really, who can afford to have anyone less than a super employees manning the business in your absence?

I know that the principles in this book will help you find, hire, train and motivate new employees and perhaps transform those who were hopeless into heroes for your business and your eventual success.

Prologue – Your Stories

As mentioned numerous times in this book, we have drawn upon the great examples, testimonials and responses to surveys from many business owners and managers throughout the world. Some are from large corporations and others come from owners of businesses with a handful of employees.

Regardless of how big your business is and how many employees you have, each owner or manager has a story to tell and experiences to share that the entire employer and small business community can draw from.

We are interested in *your* story.

The companion Website to this book is www.hopelesstohero.com.
I encourage you to share your own personal and managerial experiences as to what makes or made a significant improvement in your employees' work ethic, motivation and execution. Please submit your thoughts or experiences at www.hopelesstohero.com and we will post the information for the small business community to enjoy and benefit from.

I welcome your input.

Steve Christensen

28180434R00115

Made in the USA
Middletown, DE
05 January 2016